GUARDING THE HOME.

THE POLICE OF NEW YORK CITY
THE CITY OF BROOKLYN POLICE DEPARTMENT

Robert L. Bryan

Dedicated to Meghan, the angel always on my shoulder.

From the Author

Thank you for downloading my book detailing the history of the Brooklyn Police Department.

This is a the second book in the series highlighting the obsolete and/or lesser known police departments in New York City. The first book examined the Brooklyn Bridge Police Department. This series is a change of pace for me as most of my previous works have been memoirs regarding my police career as well as humorous works of fiction.

You can check out all my books on my Amazon Author Page. Again, thanks, and I hope you enjoy reading about this small piece of New York City policing history. I would greatly appreciate a brief review when you have completed the book.

https://www.amazon.com/Robert-L.-Bryan/e/B01LXUSALG/ref=dp_byline_cont_ebooks_1

Table of Contents

INTRODUCTION TO BROOKLYN

Since the 19th century, the perception of New York City, and in particular Brooklyn, has been characterized by the belief that residents are some of the toughest, angriest people you will ever meet. Perhaps it was all the immigrants clashing against each other. Perhaps it was the gangs that sprouted in the poorer neighborhoods. Whatever the reason, anyone from Brooklyn was someone you didn't want to mess with.

The Brooklyn character was often a badass with a hair-trigger temper, sometimes being part of the Mafia, and portraying a stereotypical attitude of a New York cab driver, at least in fiction. Even if he was one of the good guys, someone with a Brooklyn accent was bound to be tough, nonetheless. The stereotypical phantasm of the tough, poor, dim, but good-hearted lug who brutalized the English language, and especially during the World War II era he was as concerned about the Dodgers, or "Dem Bums," as he was about fighting the war.

For many Americans outside New York City this stereotypical Brooklyn character was the typical New Yorker and Brooklyn was synonymous with New York City. The concept of Brooklyn being the City's identity is not far-fetched. After all, there was a time when Brooklyn was a city.[1]

It all began just before nightfall on September 3, 1609. Henry Hudson, in his small ship, the Half Moon, cast anchor in the lower bay, at the entrance to the river that would one day bear his name. Hudson was searching for a passage to India. The Dutch, who had financed Hudson's expedition, were dissatisfied with the result of Hudson's voyage. In their estimation the discovery of new broad and fertile lands did not compensate for his failure to find a passage to India. A few shrewd merchants, however, sent a ship back to trade with the natives for skins, and the venture was so successful that, in a short time, many Dutch ships were sailing up and down the river, trading their trinkets with the natives for their valuable skins. About 1613 a trading station with a fort and a few houses was erected upon Manhattan Island. In 1623 the first colonists came to the new territory, including some who settled on the shores of Long Island.[2]

New York had been discovered and occupied more than a quarter century before any steps towards what could be considered the settlement of the city of Brooklyn were taken. In 1636 Jacob Van Corlaer, a civil officer under Director Wouyer Van Twiller in New Amsterdam, purchased from the Indians a flat of land called Castateeuw, on Long Island, between the bay of the North River and the East River. This is the earliest record of any land transaction in any area of what is now Brooklyn. More transactions followed, including the house built by William Adriaense Bennet and Jacques Bentyn, in the pioneer settlement of Gowanus, and the occupation of a tract of land on Wallabout Bay, by George Rapalje. These two settlements formed the seed from which the City of Brooklyn grew.[3]

By 1645 a public ferry operated between Manhattan and Long Island, with a small Hamlet called the Ferry springing up on the Long Island side. The Ferry, along with Gowanus and Wallabout Bay became the village of Breuckelen, named after the ancient city in Holland.[4]

The settlers quickly set up a village government, including the appointment of two Schepens, or magistrates, and a constable. The only thing known about the village government under Dutch rule was that town courts were established. When the British took control of New York, the duties of the constable, which constituted the first rules and responsibilities for police officers in Brooklyn, were listed as follows:

Whipping or punishing offenders, raising the hue and cry after murderers, manslayers, thieves, burglars: also, to apprehend without warrant such as were overtaken with drink, swearing, Sabbath breaking, vagrant persons, or night walkers.

The term "hue and cry" goes back to England in 1285. It referred to the responsibility of anyone, either a constable or a private citizen, who witnessed a crime to make hue and cry, and that the hue and cry must be kept up against the fleeing criminal from town to town and from county to county, until the felon is apprehended and delivered to the sheriff. All able-bodied men, upon hearing the shouts, were obliged to assist in the pursuit of the criminal.[5]

Constables were not allowed to take prisoners except when the offenders were caught in the act, or when their information was received from a reliable source. One of the duties was to enforce the law against Sabbath breakers – to see that the Sabbath day's calm was not disturbed by drunken brawlers. To maintain this sense of calm constables kept a close watch on tap houses to make sure they remained closed on the Sabbath.

At times, the constables were called upon to inflict the punishment of the Ducking Stool. Only women were subject to this punishment, which was imposed as a common sentence on females. The offending woman was bound to a chair and dipped in water. The theory was that this punishment was supposed to have a cooling effect upon the feminine temper.[6]

THE PILLORY AND WHIPPING-POST.

THE DUCKING-STOOL.

"Detectives" were an unknown entity in the 18th century, but Constable De B. Voise conducted the first recorded criminal investigation in Brooklyn. In 1787, a farmer named Bergen, living on Clove Road (roughly where Atlantic Avenue intersects with Classon Avenue) was robbed of his chickens. The theft was performed expertly with the thief leaving no trace or clue of his identity. De B. Voise studied the theft carefully and engaged a partner to go from house to house in the guise of being a feather-buyer. The constable's assistant finally came to the house of a respectable farmer, whose wife offered him a remarkably large number of fresh feathers for sale. Under the pretense of going to get the money to complete the sale, the assistant reported to De B. Voise who promptly returned to the house and arrested the farmer. That criminal, however, was never punished. During the first night of his incarceration in the "calaboose" or "koop," he escaped by simply kicking out the window and walking away.[7]

By the time the British took over Dutch Nieuw Nederland in 1664, six towns existed in what would become Kings County. The oldest, Gravesend, was founded by an Englishwoman, Lady Deborah Moody, in 1645. The other five were Dutch:

Boswijck (1661), "heavy woods" or "town in the woods"
Breuckelen (1646), for a town in the Netherlands
Midwout (1652), "middle woods"
Nieuw Amersfoort (1647), also for a town
Nieuw Utrecht (1657), same deal

Luckily for us, the Dutch didn't append "Nieuw" to all of their holdings in the New World, or else today 2.6 million people might live in New Brooklyn.

By 1683, when Kings County was formally established by the Colony of New York, Midwout had changed to Flatbush (from the Dutch vlacke bos, "flat woods"), Nieuw Amersfoort had become Flatlands (aiming for geographical accuracy, perhaps), and the other three names had been anglicized. Don't worry about Midwout; its legacy continues today as Midwood.

Each of the towns would set up its own grid system with proprietary naming conventions, which is why the streets and avenues in Brooklyn are so out of whack in many places. Gravesend, for example, ran its avenues east-west instead of north-south. As for the borders, they stayed in an equilibrium for nearly 150 years.

You might have noticed that not all of the territory of Kings County was originally covered. On April 14, 1827, Williamsburgh was granted a village charter within Bushwick—the start of an ascension that would last a single generation.

Brooklyn was growing by leaps and bounds; in the 1830 census, it had 12,406 people, three times its total from 20 years prior, before the introduction of rapid trans-river transport. In 1834, it upgraded itself to a city. Further north, the Village of Williamsburgh continued its growth, gobbling up even more of Bushwick's territory.

In 1840, Williamsburgh went rogue, obtaining independence from Bushwick, complete with control over its own affairs. For the first time, there were seven municipalities in Kings County.

Williamsburgh just couldn't be contained. On April 7, 1851, eleven years after becoming its own town, it declared itself the City of Williamsburgh. Including New York City, there were now three cities within a stone's throw of each other.

The change made sense: Williamsburgh was a boomtown, growing to 30,000 inhabitants in the 1850 census—six times its population in 1840. Less than a year later, on February 12, 1852, the eastern half of Flatbush seceded, calling itself the Town of New Lotts, a throwback to the area's charter. The breakaway was driven in large part by the area's huge population, thanks to an industrial-tenement area called East New York. It was a hub of German-immigrant activity in Kings County, with breweries, biergartens, newspapers, and other trappings of Deutschland.

With that, Kings County arrived at Peak Municipality: six towns and two cities. And just as quickly, an exploding population would force some mergers and acquisitions.

The first victims: the three-year-old City of Williamsburgh and its parent, the Town of Bushwick. The City of Brooklyn annexed them on April 17, 1854. The two former municipalities became known as the Eastern District of Brooklyn, and that excess 'h' fell for good from Williamsburg's name.

The next consolidation came 32 years later, in 1886, when New Lots, just a generation old, fell to the hungry monster on May 13. In her poem The New Colossus, inscribed on the base of the Statue of Liberty, Emma Lazarus confirmed Brooklyn's stature as a major city: "... her mild eyes command / The air-bridged
harbor that twin cities frame." Sometime between, Brooklyn also gained control of the land within the

southern reaches of Greenwood Cemetery and Prospect Park, shrinking Flatbush just a bit.

Brooklyn had unsuccessfully attempted to annex the rest of the county in 1873. The high-density city wanted control of suburban expansion, but the farmers in control of the towns—many descendants of original Dutch families—weren't having it.

According to an account of a hearing in the New York Times, a Mr. Bergen of New Utrecht was firmly against the idea. "The government of New-Utrecht, he said, was the least expensive; it was only an agricultural village, a long way from Brooklyn, and not in need of being included in the expenses of municipal government, at least not for the present."

The dominos came toppling in the span of a few days in 1894, as the state legislature forced consolidation on Kings County. The remaining towns were just blips.

In what the Times called the "greatest event in history of Brooklyn," Flatbush, Gravesend, and New Utrecht were absorbed into the city with immediate effect.

The effect of the absorption of the towns into Brooklyn is still felt today in a question many New Yorkers have. Why does South Brooklyn refer to Red Hook, and not to Coney Island? It doesn't seem to make sense because Coney Island is south of Red Hook. It's a question that's crossed the mind of almost every New Yorker at some point or another.

The answer is simple: as late as 1894, that area was the southern extreme of the City of Brooklyn before the towns were absorbed into Brooklyn.[8]

Flatlands was given 20 months to live. When the clock ran out, the City of Brooklyn became co-terminus with Kings County. And what a city it was! With more than a million residents, it was the third-largest city in the nation.

It was not to be, however. In what some today still call The Great Mistake of 1898, Brooklyn became a lowly borough in the consolidated City of New York. A key contributing factor was the water supply: Manhattan had the service of the seemingly limitless liquids from upstate, while Brooklyn had to rely solely on the aquifers beneath Long Island.[9]

What about policing in Brooklyn? In 1802, when her population could be numbered by hundreds, crime and vice began to make fresh and increasing inroads upon the primitive simplicity of the residents. The Town Trustees made plans to erect a "cage or watch house" and at the same time, the foreman of the fire engine companies was authorized to establish and regulate a "guard or night watch" for the prevention of crime within the limits of the town.[10]

Brooklyn grew slowly in the early years of the 19th century, and in 1825 the number of constables was increased to five and then to six in 1830.[11] Besides the constables, the number of special deputy sheriffs and public and private watchmen also increased. A secure jail was built, and a jailer was appointed by county authorities. The beginnings of a police system were seen in the establishment of a night patrol of persons other than the constables.[12]

Strangely, when Brooklyn became an actual city in 1835, there was no provision made for a police department. The new municipal authorities saved themselves the trouble of establishing a police force by appointing more watchmen and calmly recommending that citizens hire their own private security.[13]

In 1840 John S. Folk was one of the five City Marshals appointed by Cyrus P. Smith, then Mayor of the city. In 1848 the members of the Common Council after a hard-fought caucus, determined that the marshals were to act as constables, with the duty to preserve order, make arrests on criminal proceedings and attend to the service of all civil business pertaining to the Courts. From 1842 on there was increased public sentiment for police protection and the establishment of a department of the city government similar to that enjoyed by New York.

In 1850 the State Legislature passed an act providing for the election of a Chief of the Municipal Police and several police captains. John S. Folk was chosen as the first chief, and the City of Brooklyn Police Department was established.

The department was organized in the image of the New York Police Department with a superintendent as the chief of police. John Folk was the first superintendent of the Brooklyn Police Department.

Folk was a large, fearless man feared by toughs and criminals. The city divided into districts, with the more important districts called precincts and the less important as sub-precincts.[14] In 1855, the act of consolidation which united Williamsburg with Brooklyn was consummated. At this time there were seven police districts with a force of 274 men under Chief Folk. The Eighth, Ninth, and Eighteenth Wards were not included. They had special police provided at their own expense.

Policemen at this time were appointed by the Common Council with the consent of the mayor. The way it was done was as follows: The newly elected Alderman would pick out certain political favorites who had materially aided him in his elevation as one of the City

Fathers and present them to the mayor who would smile graciously, affix his signature to a formidable certificate and the appointee at once assumed the position as a guardian of the peace.

In 1859 the Metropolitan Police Act came into operation. The district comprised the counties of New York, Kings, Richmond, and Westchester. Up to this time the members of the police force in New York and Brooklyn had been controlled by the local authorities but now five commissioners were appointed together with the Mayors of New York and Brooklyn, controlled the police affairs of four counties.[15]

The new force was made up largely of those whose political tendencies coincided with the commission's. Appointments were made to the Brooklyn force to raise the total number to 368. Additionally, there were fourteen men specially detailed as the Atlantic Dock Squad, whose mission was protecting the docks and who were paid by the Atlantic Dock Company. There was a Sanitary Squad of eight officers, including a sergeant, detailed to execute the orders and protect the employees of the Board of Health. There were also about forty special officers who were hired and paid by private citizens to protect their warehouses and factories. Under Superintendent Folk the old discipline was maintained, despite the demoralizing influence of the political agendas brought into being by the commission.

1858-59 was an uneventful period. James Nye was President of the Metropolitan Police Commission with James S. T. Stranahan as Brooklyn Commissioner and John Folk as deputy superintendent.

In 1860 Brooklyn was still rapidly growing with nineteen wards and a population of 266,000. The Police

Department was still part of the Metropolitan Police System and Thomas R.B. Stillman was the new President of the Commission.

A captain, sergeants, and as many patrolmen required were assigned to a precinct based on the size and population of the area. The result of the new police force was an enormous increase in the number of arrests and a great decrease in the number of reported crimes. Superintendent Folk was one of the first police administrators who espoused the virtues of crime prevention over police reacting to crimes already committed.[16]

The word precinct comes from the Latin precinctum meaning "enclosure, boundary line." A precinct is an area that has a clear boundary line around it, making it easier for the police to know where a crime is taking place, or where you should go to vote. The word precinct has also come to mean police headquarters in a particular district.[17]

The early years of the department passed without any noteworthy events. The force became disciplined and trustworthy. Worthless and incompetent policemen were weeded out and intelligent and capable officers were promoted into more responsible positions. As time went on, however, it became clear that the Metropolitan Policing System was not beneficial for effective, honest policing.[18]

The drumbeat was getting louder for the arrival of the Civil War and politicians of the worst type dominated the landscape, leaving no stone unturned to ensure every possible advantage for their organizations. It was through the efforts of unscrupulous men such as these that the bill was passed placing the policing of New York in the hands of an irresponsible commission who were no better than the typical corrupt politician of the time. The commission exercised despotic power over three thousand police officers, and control over seven million dollars per year. The commission could control elections and dictate to the people what candidates their conventions should nominate.[19]

The New York Draft Riots occurred in July 1863, when the anger of working-class New Yorkers over a new federal draft law during the Civil War sparked five days of some of the bloodiest and most destructive rioting in U.S. history. Hundreds of people were killed, many more seriously injured, and African Americans were often the target of the rioters' violence.

Facing a dire shortage of manpower in early 1863, Lincoln's government passed a strict new conscription law, which made all male citizens between 20 and 35 and all unmarried men between 35 and 45 subject to military duty. Though all eligible men were entered into a lottery, they could buy their way out of harm's way by hiring a substitute or paying $300 to the government. At the time, that sum was the yearly salary for the average American worker, making avoiding the draft impossible for all but the wealthiest of men. Compounding the issue, African Americans were exempt from the draft, as they were not considered citizens.

Riots over the draft occurred in other cities, including Detroit and Boston, but nowhere as badly as in New York. Anti-war newspapers published attacks on the new draft law, fueling the mounting anger of white workers leading up to the city's first draft lottery on July 11, 1863.

By far the worst violence was reserved for African American men, a number of whom were lynched or beaten to death with shocking brutality. In all, the published death toll of the New York City draft riots was 119 people, though estimates of the actual number of people killed reached as high as 1,200.[20]

The horrors of the rioting in New York City seemed to be about to be copied in Brooklyn, but the determination of Folk and the municipal authorities, as well as the courage and discipline of the men of the Brooklyn Police Department saved Brooklyn from the horrendous scenes playing out across the river.

The expense of the Civil War required cuts to the city's budget, and in 1864 the size of the Brooklyn Police Department was reduced to 287 men. In the meantime, the inefficiency of the Metropolitan District Police Law was being felt. Police appointments of the most objectionable candidates were being made to the Brooklyn force to placate New York and out of town politicians. In some instances, these new appointees could scarcely read or write, had not been in the country long enough to vote, and knew nothing of New York law or Brooklyn geography. With the department's administration being across the river in Manhattan, during the thirteen years in which the law was in force, the Brooklyn authorities knew about as much about their own police as they did about those of Chicago or any other distant city. No reports were made to the mayor, and no local record was either made or maintained. People seeking records of the Brooklyn Police during this period could not look in the Brooklyn archives, but instead had to visit the Mulberry Street headquarters in Manhattan or the archives of the state capital in Albany.

In 1869 the Board of Metropolitan Police was reorganized. Thomas C. Acton resigned the office of commissioner in April and was succeeded by Henry Smith. Commissioner Joseph S. Bosworth was elected President of the Board. Two new sub-precincts were created, and the ranks of the police department increased to 446 men.

A new phenomenon that began to appear in police reports were the number of nightly lodgers. During that era, it was a noble and charitable practice for the police department to provide lodging at the station houses to those who requested. Up until this time, however, the requests for lodging usually came from workingmen out of a job, the sick, disabled, and indigent elderly. By 1869 the lodgers had significantly changed. Although there were less requests for lodging, those making the requests were primarily tramps, drunkards, sneakthieves, and vagabonds. The rooms in the station houses became so filthy that the decent citizens seeking shelter were driven away, preferring to walk the streets or beg for the money to secure a room in a ten-cent hotel. Some even went so far as to commit an insignificant offense in order to be placed in a jail cell which was preferrable to the accommodations at the station houses.

Sergeant David V. W. Lawson, of the First Precinct, provided insights into the problem with providing overnight lodging at the station houses in 1877. The 46-year-old sergeant was described as medium height and build, with a dark complexion.

In speaking of the "evils" of city life, Sgt. Lawson said, "We try to discourage tramp lodgers as much as we can. We find that it fosters drunkenness to give the tramp free lodgings this time of the year. There are a lot of tramps in the city who go about begging in the daytime.

Every one of them pick up enough to eat, and a few nickels here and there. By the time night comes they have enough money to buy a night's lodging in a cheap lodging house, but they prefer to spend their cash for stale beer and bad whiskey. When they are comfortably loaded, they go to the station houses to get free lodgings. A regular tramp will not go to sleep with money in his pocket, if he can help it. In cold winter weather I hate to turn tramps away, but from April to October it doesn't seem to hurt them to sleep in trucks and hallways. Lately I have adopted a plan to discourage station house bums. I put them under arrest, and they are sent to the work-house or penitentiary."

While the sergeant was being interviewed the door opened, and a youth thinly clad entered to ask for lodgings. He did not look as if he had been drinking and was a stranger to the sergeant. "I have been looking for work, and haven't got enough money for a bed," he said.

"How much have you got?"

"Six cents." He took from his pocket a copy of the Eagle, a nickel and a cent.

"Did you buy that paper?"

"Yes. I have just been to answer an advertisement from a man near here, but the place was already filled." He pointed out to the sergeant the advertisement for an able - bodied young man, wanted at a place not far away.

"That will do, we will give you as good lodgings as we have in the house, and here is something for your breakfast." The sergeant added a silver coin to the stranger's six cents and sent him back to the lodging-room.

Another man, dirty and shabby, had slid into the station, and was making for the lodging-room too, with the easy self-consciousness of a regular lodger, when the sergeant stopped him. "Hold on a minute, Johnny. I want to talk to you. Do you remember promising me when you were here last time that you would stop drinking?"

"Did stop-several times," said the smiling tramp.

A ring of the bell called the doorman and a policeman in uniform. The Sergeant wrote down the tramp's name, age, nationality, and the charge " intoxication," and said, "Lock him up." Turning over the leaves of the blotter, the sergeant said, "That makes the seventh tramp in the cells to night, and it isn't ten o'clock yet."

On April 5, 1870, the State legislature passed a bill making the police department in the City of Brooklyn and independent organization, and on April 28th Daniel D. Briggs and Isaac Van Anden were appointed Police Commissioners. A new police headquarters was established at Court and Livingston Streets. The vast majority of the police force who had been appointed under the Metropolitan Police Commission were retained, regardless of political affiliations, and all the precincts were renumbered.

In 1872 the Board of Police was again reorganized with the mayor reappointing Daniel Briggs and adding General James Jourdan and Sigmund Kaufman to the board. The addition of another member to the board was a political move. The mayor of Brooklyn was a democrat, but the republicans had seized control of New York State government. A bill was passed increasing the police commission to three members with the mayor (democrat), auditor and comptroller (republicans) each making one appointment. This ensured that the commission would be republican in character.

Prior to the 1870s Brooklyn was known as the "City of Homes." What little business it did was supplied by retail stores, breweries, and a few factories. The crowding of Manhattan soon drew attention to the low rents and superb accommodations of its sparsely populated neighbor. Building was done on a large scale, with factories, warehouses, and wholesalers springing up all along the extended waterfront and the banks of Newtown Creek and the Gowanus Canal. The increase in commercial activity was accompanied by a corresponding increase in crime. An increased workload was thrust upon the police department. From time to time there were some increases made to police manpower and infrastructure, but these increases usually proved inadequate to keep up with the growing demands of the municipality.[21]

In 1898 it was all over when Brooklyn became a borough in the Greater New York City and the Brooklyn Police Department was absorbed into the New York City Police Department.

That completes a brief history of Brooklyn and of the City of Brooklyn Police Department. But that is not what this book is about. I wanted to tell a story of what it was like to be a Brooklyn Policeman, and the day to day issues these men faced. This would seem like a daunting task, considering that the Brooklyn Police Department ceased to exist in 1898. But then I discovered the Brooklyn newspapers. There were several daily papers, including the Brooklyn edition of the World , a morning daily ; the Brooklyn Daily Eagle, Times, Standard - Union , Citizen and Freie Presse. Especially during the latter part of the 19th century, they reported in great depth and detail on the workings and personnel of the police department.

Back in the 19th century there was not the instant communication resulting in a news cycle that could change by the minute. Even with the advent of the telegraph news from outside of a local area took an extended period of time to be reported in detail. That is why the media reported local stories in such great detail. Name, address, physical description, manner of dress, social status and affiliations, hobbies, and standing among neighbors were commonly used in descriptions of subjects in stories, regardless of the nature of the article.

The police department held a special place for the news reporters of the era. The relationship between the police and the newspapers was different than today. In the latter part of the 19th century the police and the newspapers seemed to be working in something of a partnership.

In his 1887 book, Brooklyn's Guardians, William E.S. Fales describes the police relationship with the newspapers. "All of the Brooklyn newspapers have been of vast use to the police, as well as to the public, for their successful efforts in attacking the evils which, always incidental to the growth of a great city, have from time to time blemished the fair record of the City of Churches. The Eagle, ever since its birth, has waged war to the knife against gambling dens, low dives and houses of questionable character. So zealous and so thorough has it been in its good work that scarcely any disreputable place has ever been started within the city limits but what within thirty days thereafter it has been exposed in the news items, denounced in an editorial or described in a special notice to the police.[23]

An interesting phenomenon I found regarding the news reporting of the police during the 19th century which is vastly different than it is today was the very obvious pro-police stance in the reporting. That didn't mean, however, that reporters wouldn't take shots at the department and individual policemen when they deserved it. Those negative shots were sharp, biting, sarcastic, and in many instances, humorous.

Most of the detailed reporting on the police I found was in the latter part of the 19th century. So, this is the story of the Brooklyn Police mainly from the 1870s up until the department merged into a newly consolidated New York City Police Department in 1898.

One of the more fascinating aspects of the press coverage of the police department was the detail in which the members of the department were covered. Today, it is very common to find profiles of commissioners, chiefs, and precinct commanders, but the Brooklyn newspapers of the late 19th century provided in depth profiles of the members of the police department right down to the ordinary patrolman. In some cases, I felt as if I was reading a scorecard describing a baseball team rather than the members of a police department. Incidentally, there will be much more about baseball and the Brooklyn Police Department later. For now, let's stick with the Fourth Precinct of the Brooklyn Police Department.

Brooklyn Policeman escorts prisoner to court

FOURTH PRECINCT PROFILE

The 88th Precinct of the New York City Police Department is located on the southwest corner of Classon and DeKalb Avenues. It is an impressive example of Romanesque Revival style architecture and provides a glimpse of the history of the Brooklyn Police Department. The 88th Precinct began its policing history as the Fourth Precinct of the Brooklyn Police Department. The building's present location replaced an earlier station house at Myrtle and Vanderbilt Avenues. Following the consolidation of Greater New York in 1898 the Fourth Precinct became known as the 156th Precinct, and later the 96th Precinct.

The Fourth Precinct was one of the first police precincts organized in Brooklyn. It covered the aristocratic neighborhood around Clinton Avenue and Fort Greene Park containing a wide mix in the class of the population.

Late 19th century station houses were generally planned with various rooms for uniformed officers, cells for short-term prisoners, and stables. The muster room, where officers were given their daily duties, was usually located in the front of the main building, near the entrance. It had a large sergeant's desk and adjoined the captain's office and private quarters. On the upper floors were the section rooms, including dormitories and washrooms for the patrolmen, who frequently worked 16-hour shifts. There was an independent cell block, temporary accommodations for the homeless or drunk, and a separate structure for horses and the "hoodlum" wagon.

When the new Fourth Precinct station house at Classon and DeKalb opened in 1890, it had 64 officers, including a captain, four sergeants, and 44 patrolmen. This number increased gradually, reaching 80 in 1917.

In May 1898 all 80 police precincts in the newly consolidated New York City Police Department were redistricted and renumbered. At this time, the Fourth Precinct became the 56th Precinct. By 1908 it was changed to the 156th Precinct, and then to the 96th Precinct in 1918. Since about 1930 it has remained the 88th precinct.[24]

On Sunday morning, June 25, 1876, Brooklynites, like the rest of the nation were preparing for the centennial celebration marking the one hundredth birthday of the United States. Approximately two thousand miles from Brooklyn, however, there was no celebration. On a hill above the Little Bighorn River General George Armstrong Custer lay with 265 members of his command. News of the massacre would not reach Brooklyn until July 5th. On this hot, lazy summer morning, readers of the Brooklyn Daily Eagle were treated to a feature story profiling the members of the Fourth Precinct of the Brooklyn Police Department.

The story detailed how the police of the Fourth Precinct covered the aristocratic portion of the city called "the Hill," where sneak thieves lurked in the summertime when the affluent residents were on vacation in the country.

Oliver B. Leich was the officer in command of the Fourth Precinct. He formerly had command of the Ninth and Twelfth Precincts. In appearance Captain Leich was described as not prepossessing. His face, where not covered by gray whiskers, and a moustache was suspiciously red in color and his manner was not apt to induce a stranger or acquaintance for that matter, to take to him. Before being appointed to his present position, Captain Leich ran for the assembly in the ninth district against the Hon. John McGroarty. He was not elected, by a large majority. Off and on Mr. Leich had been attached to the police force for a number of years. Approximately a year earlier he was nearly discharged for speaking disrespectfully of his superiors.

Apparently, the Captain was not a popular figure. The article noted that neither with the public nor the majority of men under him was Captain Leich a favorite, and if he was to leave the force tomorrow there would be few to regret him.

Sergeant Charles Storm had eleven years on the force, and during that time had done much to commend himself. Before going to the Fourth Mr. Storm served in the Seventh and Eighth Precincts. He was a sergeant for four years. Some time ago, while arresting a burglar, one of the thief's pals assaulted him with a jimmy, and Sgt. Storm was severely wounded. The mark of the blow was still plainly discernable upon his forehead. Sergeant Storm assisted to capture Pellicer, one of the murderers of Otero.

The Otero murder was an infamous crime in Brooklyn in 1865. Jose Garcia Otero came to New York after winning a large lottery prize in Cuba with the intention of investing money in a New York theatre. Otero took a room at the Hotel de Barcelona on Great Jones Street, and it was there he met Jose Gonzales, who had been boarding at the hotel for some days. During the day on November 22nd, Gonzalez accompanied Otero into Brooklyn where they spent time at Evans's drinking house at the corner of Myrtle Avenue and Canton Street. At about 9 pm they were joined by another man, accomplice Theodore Pellicer, and all three drank profusely. When they left the saloon they went in the direction of a nearby park. In this park, surrounded by occupied dwellings, the murder was committed without attracting attention. A few minutes afterward someone passing through the park stumbled over a body which he supposed to be that of a drunken man. A closer inspection revealed that the man was dead and his body frightfully mutilated. The police, upon their arrival at the spot, found near the body a dirk, two razors, and a pair of gloves. The latter were cut across the fingers, and evidently belonged to one of the assassins with whom the murdered man had struggled.[25]

Captain Waddy arresting Gonzalez

John Corr had been on the police force seventeen years and had always been rated as a first-class officer. Corr was for a long time attached to the Sanitary Squad (more on the Sanitary Squad later). He was described as a good-looking Irishman with black hair and a well-trimmed moustache. Corr had been a sergeant for the past six years during which time he had done duty in the Fourth Precinct.

Sergeant John Barr was a six-footer, and a chin whisker decorated his not unhandsome face. He was a good officer and went to the Fourth from the First Precinct. He had also done duty in the Eighth and Tenth Precincts and in each place, he was considered a faithful and conscientious officer. Barr was appointed sergeant six years ago.

Sergeant Kelly sported a neat, light-colored moustache. He had done fifteen years police duty, six of which he had served as a sergeant. He was genial, good hearted, and well-liked by all with whom he came in contact.

Officer Edward Scott was the terror of lawbreakers in general. He was a fat, red faced fellow, and was always laughing. With his club Scott was an expert, whether sounding an alarm or bringing it in contact with an offender's head. Wow! I don't think you'll see those type accolades in any of today's media.

A quick word about sounding an alarm with a club because you will hear about this tactic numerous times throughout the book. There was no radio communication during the 19th century so policemen would pound their clubs on the sidewalk or any solid object to cause a loud noise. Any other policeman who heard the sound of the club would recognize it as an alarm signal and run to the sound. I joined the New York City Transit Police

Department in 1981, and during my first months on the job I had an incident where a sergeant who had come on the job during the 1950s became outraged at me. Why was this sergeant so angry? On a midnight shift I was working alone patrolling an underground subway station in Lower Manhattan. It was very quiet but off in the distance I heard a faint "rapping" sound. The rapping went on for several minutes before stopping. Five minutes later, the red-faced sergeant appeared in front of me and bellowed. "Why didn't you respond to my call?"

"What call?" I asked.

The sergeant took out his night stick and began banging it on the concrete station floor. "Didn't you hear this?"

"Oh, that was you?" I replied.

The sergeant turned away with a look of disgust on his face and departed the station. How was I supposed to know that in 1981 he was still using a tactic popular with the police in the 1880s. Now, back to Officer Scott.

It was Scott who did detective duty in the case of Hallinan, charged with the murder of William Russell in the early part of 1876, four years after the commission of the crime. Scott traced the murderer to Chicago, and there he learned that he had left for San Francisco, where a short time after he was arrested.

Not all of the profiles in the article were complimentary. About a year before the article, Scott was fined $50 for striking a politician who interfered with him in the discharge of his duty.

His superiors said Thomas Allen was a good officer. I suppose you could say that assessment of Officer Allen is concise and right to the point.

The article had a lot more to say about Detective Riggs. Detective Riggs, next to ex-chief of police Matsel of New York, excels at thieves' slang. This is his style: "Jimmy, he faked the super from his nibs. I was on the lay. Nosey, when he saw the coppers, squealed and gave the kid away and if it wasn't for his Moll I'd have put the bracelets on Jimmy. He got cornered soon after and is doing a tener in the jug at Peoria. Jimmy was very fly but he got full of budge and the coppers nabbed him."

Riggs ability as a detective was very often displayed in the arrest of small boys for playing ball in the streets and drunken women.

Price, Rigg's partner, was not a good detective, except in theory. Since he had been on the force, he had arrested a few petty thieves, and that was about all he had to his credit. In appearance he looked like a Jersey farmer: his straw-colored moustache set off a pair of peculiar hued red cheeks. Like Riggs he imagined that he was "the detective of Brooklyn" and like Riggs his opinion of himself was far stretched.

Officer Thomas Baker was the owner of a black moustache, and it was conceded that he was the handsomest man in the Fourth Precinct. Tom was also a faithful officer.

Thomas E. Borie was very short in stature. That's it! – short in stature. I wonder how Officer Borie felt picking up the Eagle on that Sunday morning and looking for his profile, only to find that he was – short in stature.

Officer Dan Hall had never done anything to distinguish himself. This description is even worse. Hall was "nothing" – not even short in stature.

Officers Shandley and Shaughnessy should not be mentioned separately, as they always worked together.

Both men did duty in Justice Riley's court, and they were
without doubt, taken together, the two best officers on the
Brooklyn Police Force. They had done considerable
detective duty and never slipped up in a case. In fact, they
exceled the regular detectives. Shaughnessy and Shandley
arrested Henry A. Solomon, the embezzler, on a warrant
when the detectives were hunting the city for him. In
appearance both officers were fine looking young fellows.
Shandley's upper lip was covered with a coal black
moustache while Shaughnessy's was a blond. In other
courts, it required five or six officers to do the work
performed by these two men.

Larry Delahanty was a very small fellow. He stole
on the force. At a fire, a policeman laid down his coat;
Larry picked it up and fell in with the other officers. It
was thought that he will do detective duty on the Hill this
summer because of the ease with which he can steal into a
home through the keyhole, after burglars. Notwithstanding
his size, Larry was a good reliable officer. After this
profile, calling Officer Borie short in stature doesn't seem
so bad. It seems that the author is alluding to the fact that
Delahanty was so small and didn't meet the department's
physical requirement, that he must have used some
fraudulent means to get on the force. But wait a minute –
he's a good, reliable officer.

Thomas Dolan was an old officer who made a fair
policeman. There's a ringing endorsement.

John Martin had been on the force five-years, and he
was a good, faithful officer who minds his own business.
In all my years in law enforcement I never received or
prepared an evaluation that included the category of
"minding own business." Who knows, maybe it is a
behavioral characteristic that should be evaluated?

James McKean was a new officer of whom nothing can be said beyond that he devoted considerable of his wages to fines imposed by the Commissioners. I would think reporting that the officer spends a lot of his pay on department fines is saying a lot.

Alec C. Pearsall had done three years' service and had never done anything brilliant. I am going to stick up for Officer Pearsall and look at the glass as being half full. He also had never done anything stupid.

William A. Perine had been on the force ten years. He had a habit of losing his club and was generally assisted by the roundsman in his search for it.

William Quigley had worn a shield six months and as yet had done nothing to distinguish himself. I guess this reporter never had a mother like mine who said, "If you can't say something nice about a person, don't say anything."

Bernard Regan, in the language of a brother officer, was a "red mouth." As hard as I tried, I could not find an exact meaning and context for "red mouth." I know it was not a compliment, and I will guess to say that it was either a gossiper or a loudmouth, or perhaps a combination of the two. Regan was a very political person and claimed to be personally acquainted with every person of note from Governor Tilden down to Henry Slocum. If Regan let politics take care of themselves and attended to his duty, he might probably make a fair officer

Roundsman James Shepard had been on the force fourteen years, nearly all of which time he had done on duty in the fourth precinct. He was a good officer, and would be even a better one, were it not that he had a very loose tongue. Perhaps Shepard should have gotten some lessons from Officer Martin about minding his own business.{26}

Eleven years later a much "fluffier" description of the Fourth Precinct and its personnel was provided by Fales in Guardians of Brooklyn.

In 1887 the Fourth Precinct was described as one of the pleasantest precincts in Brooklyn. It covered the aristocratic neighborhood about Clinton Avenue and Fort Greene Park, and contained a mixed population described as the best and worst classes. Most of the police problems originated mainly from the district north of Myrtle Avenue from an area called "under the Hill." The station house was situated on the corner of Myrtle and Vanderbilt Avenues. It was a three-story brick building, with an extension for the cells and lodging- rooms. Under the Metropolitan Policing System it was known as the Forty-Fourth Precinct, but under the original Municipal Police and after the reorganization which followed the repeal of the Metropolitan Act, it again became Fourth Precinct. Its boundaries were Hudson Avenue to Franklin Avenue, and Flushing Avenue to Fulton Avenue.

Captain William J. McKelvey was the commanding officer in 1887. He was born on March 12, 1842 and was described as stout and of medium height. When the Civil War began Captain McKelvey was one of the first to volunteer as a soldier, joining the Tenth New York Volunteers. After two years the regiment was sent to Philadelphia where it was disbanded, and Sergeant McKelvey was among those discharged. He returned to New York, and at once began to form a company of volunteers of which he intended to take command, and again engage in the conflict between the North and South. The government was slow in furnishing the necessary equipment, and while Sergeant McKelvey and his volunteers were lying idle in New York the draft riots broke out. McKelvey and his men assisted the police in putting down the rioters, and Thomas C. Acton, then President of the Metropolitan Police Force, noticed the gallant conduct of Sergeant McKelvey, and afterwards offered him a position on the police force. He accepted the offer and became a patrolman, attached to the Thirty-Ninth Precinct. He was promoted to the office of roundsman in 1866, but resigned from the police department in 1870 to enter the oil business in New York. In the winter of 1872, a fire destroyed all of Mr. McKelvey's business, and he came to Brooklyn. In September of 1872 he secured a position on the Brooklyn Police Force, under General Jourdan. He served as a patrolman of the Tenth Precinct for four months, when he secured a place in the Telegraph Department. In 1883 he was made drill captain. On the 17th of January 1885, Captain Willmarth, of the Fourth Precinct, retired, and Captain McKelvey took his place.

WILLIAM J. McKELVEY,
Captain.

Charles Strong, of the Fourth Precinct, was born in 1829. On the 18th of May 1865, he secured an appointment as patrolman on the Metropolitan Police Force. He did good work during his service in the ranks and on the 20th of June 1872, he was promoted to the office of sergeant.

Sergeant William P. Kelly was born on the 22nd of January 1833. On July 20, 1861, he was appointed patrolman by Commissioner Thomas C. Acton, of the Metropolitan Police. After serving for eight years in New York, he was transferred to the Brooklyn branch. On June 30, 1870, he was promoted to the position of sergeant, and assigned to the Fourth Precinct, July 24th, 1871. His record was excellent.

Sergeant Stephen Martin was forty-two years of age. He became a patrolman on January 20th, 1868, and was on July 16th, 1875, appointed a sergeant. Sergeant Martin was intimately acquainted with the criminal classes of both New York and Brooklyn and could tell many thrilling stories of their deeds and misdeeds. In speaking of crimes, he said, "I notice a growing decrease in the amount of violence and brutality. The sneak thief is replacing the highwayman and burglar. The river thief, once so powerful an element in crime, is now almost extinct. Yet in my time he was one of our most dangerous foes."

Sergeant Thomas F. Mande was born on the eleventh of December 1859. On April 4th, 1882, he was appointed a patrolman. He was promoted to roundsman December 5th, 1885, and on the eighth of January 1887, he advanced one more step up the ladder and became a sergeant of the Fourth Precinct. Sergeant Mande performed good service as an officer and deserved all the honors that were bestowed upon him by the city.

The roundsmen attached to the Fourth Precinct were William Knipe and George W. Raynor. The detectives of the Fourth Precinct were Thomas Shaughnessy and Joseph Price. Shaughnessy served with distinction as a soldier through the great war and joined the Police Force in 1868. Price was also a veteran, not of the army, but of the navy. Both were officers of merit, and were held in high esteem [27]

OFFICER EDWARD SCOTT

I would like to return to Officer Edward Scott. You remember him, don't you? He was the expert with his club. The story of Officer Scott is fascinating, and ultimately, tragic.

Edward Scott was born in Ireland in 1841. Before becoming a police officer, he worked as a laborer at the Tobacco Inspection Stores. He was appointed to the Brooklyn Police Department on July 5th, 1874.[28]

On August 16th, 1875, Scott had some type of confrontation with a private watchman. The next morning around 7 AM Michael Smith, an Attaché of the Board of City Works was waiting for a car on Atlantic Street when Scott walked by on patrol. "Mr. Officer, how did you and the private watchman make out on the run in you had?"

"What did you say?" Scott asked.

Smith repeated the question and Scott then made three dashes at him with his club but didn't hit him as he said, "You are a damn loafer, and I will make you eat this stick."

Scott then struck Smith with his fist knocking him several feet into the street. Scott claimed he reacted the way he did because Smith had made some previous remark about dying his moustache. Smith said he had never spoken to Scott before. James McGuire, a witness, corroborated Smith's story and said there was no justification for Scott to strike him.

Scott said he was a policeman for 12-months and knew Smith by sight only. Scott said the remark Smith made was "I heard that policemen were killing one another last night."

Scott said he walked over to Smith and said, "You hear more than your prayer; you had better attend to your own business, or I will make you; let me attend to mine.

Smith then said, "You are looking for what you will get around here; you will get your red moustache dyed redder than what it already is."

Scott said, "Get out of here you loafer," while giving Smith a chuck on the breast with the back of his hand.

Smith denied these statements. Scott was found guilty and fined $50 or three months in jail.[29]

I suppose the moral to this story is to never comment on a man's moustache. I found it remarkable that Scott could be fined, sentenced to jail and still keep his job as a police officer. More remarkable was the fact that the incident with the politician was not Scott's first brush with department discipline. Several months earlier Scott was fined five days' pay for going into a house on New Year's Day, wishing the folks a happy new year and taking a drink of wine.[30]

I could not find any record to show whether Officer Scott actually served his jail time. In November of 1875, however, he was back at it again. Officer Scott arrested Thomas Mehan and Thomas Kelly for acting in a disorderly manner on Atlantic Street. Kelly swore that they made no noise except talking in a loud manner. He said that Officer Scott caught him and beat him over the head with his club. Justice Walsh discharged the boys and reprimanded the officer for using his club when there was no occasion for it.[31]

After all the negative incidents, Edward Scott's big break came from an incident that occurred long before he became a police officer. While working on the docks before joining the police force, he became acquainted with a longshoreman named John Hallinan who worked on one of the Furman Street docks. On June 27th, 1871, Hallinan became involved in a dispute with a co-worker named William Russell. Russell had accused Hallinan of not contributing his share to the purchase of ice for their pail of drinking water. Russell called Hallinan a "Damn mean shoe boy," and struck him with a barrel stave. Russell died of his injuries within 24-hours, and Hallinan was able to elude capture.[32]

The crime gradually faded from public memory and was only rekindled five years after the crime in a startling fashion. The crime never faded from the mind of the son of William Russell, and when he found out someone fitting Hallinan's description was taken into custody in New York, he rushed to the city to make an identification. Young Russell positively identified the man in custody as his father's murderer, but Chief of Police Campbell had his doubts. Chief Campbell was informed that Brooklyn Policeman Edward Scott had known Hallinan and was very familiar with his appearance, so Officer Scott was brought to the jail to view a lineup of ten prisoners, including the man thought to be Hallinan. After viewing the lineup Scott said he was certain that Hallinan was not in the group. Chief Campbell commented to Scott that it was amazing that Hallinan could not be tracked down in five years. Scott told the Chief that it would seem very possible to be able to track Hallinan down, at which point Campbell pulled Scott off his duties in the Fourth Precinct and detailed him to work exclusively on finding Hallinan.

Scott found some friends of Hallinan in Brooklyn who told him that Hallinan's wife worked at Rudolph's Store on Broadway in New York. Scott learned from the janitor at the store that the woman in question left New

York for Providence, Rhode Island, leaving her child in a Roman Catholic orphanage in New York. Scott also learned from the store janitor that the woman thought to be Hallinan's wife had employed a stranger to write a letter for her to a man named Kenefick, who was employed in the Providence Locomotive works. Scott traveled to Providence and met Kenefick and the woman from Rudolph's Store but found to his disgust that she was not Hallinan's wife. Scott next learned that certain parties in New York had received letters from a friend of Hallinan's in Chicago. Chief Campbell gave Scott a letter of introduction to the Chicago Chief of Police and sent him to Chicago. After days of tireless work Scott discovered that Hallinan had worked for two years driving a streetcar on the west side of the city, but that a year ago he had left with his wife and family for San Francisco, and that he was driving a streetcar there. Scott sent a telegraph to Chief Campbell informing him that he had tracked Hallinan to San Francisco. Campbell sent Scott a telegraph telling him to wait before leaving for San Francisco until he could find out whether Russell's family was willing to incur the expense of transporting Hallinan back to Brooklyn. A week later Campbell sent a telegraph directing Scott to return to Brooklyn. Chief Campbell telegraphed all the pertinent information to the San Francisco Police and about a week later Hallinan was arrested, with San Francisco footing the bill for his return to Brooklyn. In singing the praises of Officer Scott, the newspapers speculated that the officer would probably not be returning to his post duty again.[33]

The predictions of the reporters were wrong because only a few months later, on the night of July 1, 1876, Officer Edward Scott was again on duty on Myrtle

Avenue, walking up and down the post discharging his duty.[34] A little after midnight Grocer August Schliemann was closing his shop when he exchanged a greeting with Officer Scott who was walking by.[35] Shortly before 1 AM Scott strolled toward the corner of Steuben Street and Myrtle Avenue. Gathered around a pump on that corner were the Jackson Hollow Gang, a group of young men who regularly terrorized the neighborhood.[36]

The Jackson Hollow Gang was one of the most prevalent and certainly long-lasting gangs in Brooklyn. The area formerly known as "Jackson Hollow" was the gang's home turf. An 1858 article in the New York Times, which was essentially a crude census of the squatters in the area was described thusly, "Upon Grand Avenue, North of Myrtle Avenue, there are 44 shanties having 230 inmates... Between DeKalb and Lafayette Avenues, 20 shanties having 90 inmates... A total of 340 shanties having 1,427 inhabitants of the Hollow... How this large number contrive to subsist at all is a wonder." It had many gangs, but one in particular dominated from their original arrival in the 1840s due to The Great Hunger in Ireland to the turn of the century when they were still committing crimes in Brooklyn, the Jackson Hollow Gang.[37]

In front of James Carberry's liquor store some of the gang were scuffling among themselves while the rest were applauding and cheering in a rowdy fashion. Scott approached the twelve to fifteen in the group and said quietly, "Hey boys, you'll have to move away from here."

The officer's direction was met with boisterous laughter prompting Scott to swing his club to drive them off.[38] Scott ordered the group to move on and they cursed at him. As Scott approached them someone in the crowd said, "Let's give it to him.[39]

Gang member James Whalehan said, "We take possession of this corner," before continuing to curse at the officer.[40]

The gang didn't run but instead surrounded Scott. Scott saw that he was in trouble and tried to break through with his club. Someone in the gang yelled, "Get that son of a bitch," at which time Scott was struck a blow to the face and the back of the neck. The gang set upon Scott, but he fought them off. He may have succeeded when someone threw a large stone that hit Scott on the left temple.[41]

August Schliemann saw someone fall among a group of men near the pump on the corner of Myrtle Avenue and Steuben Street. Schliemann saw Hubert Conroy dragging Officer Scott along the sidewalk. He asked Conroy what he was doing, and Conroy said he was taking the officer to the drug store to get help.[42]

Hugh Conroy was standing on the corner of Myrtle Avenue and Grand Street when he heard a disturbance a block away. He walked over and observed Officer Scott in the center of a crowd. He heard Scott say, "Boys, clear the sidewalk and let the folks go by." Conroy said the words had just left Scott's mouth when someone struck him with a large paving stone and Scott fell. Conroy rushed into the crowd and picked up Scott. He used Scott's club to "rap for assistance." and carried him to a nearby drug store.[43]

Officers Skelton, Van Brunt and Gelhart responded and the gang fled.[44] James Carberry, the owner of the liquor store at 523 Myrtle Avenue where the incident occurred, said he knew nothing because his store was closed and he was asleep inside the store. John Flood was

at the drug store when Conroy brought Scott inside. Flood
then walked to the corner of Myrtle Avenue and Steuben
Street where he ran into James Whalehan. Whalehan
asked Flood if Scott was badly hurt. When Flood said yes,
Whalehan said it served Scott right and that he brought it
on himself because he had been insulting men and woman
on his post. Flood also said that Whalehan said both he
and Hurley struck Scott and when Scott came at them
Hurley hit him with a large stone.[45]

Scott was taken from drug store to the Fourth
Precinct Station House. Police Surgeon Wilson responded
and examined Officer Scott. Wilson said the wound did
not appear to be dangerous, so Scott was taken by
ambulance to his home at 205 Fulton Street.46]

Monday evening Officer Scott travelled to the
station house and told the sergeant in charge that he was
ready to go on post. As he was talking to the sergeant
Scott began to experience severe pain in his head, so the
sergeant told him to go home. Surgeon Kissam responded
to Scott's home and directed him to the hospital
immediately, but he died shortly after he arrived at the
hospital. The cause of death was listed as compression of
the brain [47]

22-year old John Hurley and nine other members of
the Jackson Hollow Gang were arrested and charged with
Scott's murder.[48] The 35-year old Scott was married
with five children. He had worked two years on the
Brooklyn Police Department.[49]

On the day of the funeral Officer Scott lay in a
rosewood casket in his home, the casket adorned with a
floral cross with the words "We mourn our loss." Around
the casket stood the weeping wife and children. A
policeman stood at the door to the residence and permitted

but a few to enter. When the hearse and carriage drove up, a large crowd gathered outside the residence. The captains of police and all off duty Brooklyn Police officers gathered at police headquarters in full dress uniform. The coffin was still open when it was brought out of the house allowing police to march past and give a final look at their brother officer. The line then formed for the march to the cemetery to the tap of the muffled drums of the 23rd Regiment's band and drum corps. The full Fourth Precinct surrounded the hearse with Captain Leich and his sergeants walking in the rear. Along the route the sidewalk was jammed with people watching the 250 policemen in the procession. The line of march to Holy Cross cemetery passed the scene of the incident at Myrtle Avenue and Steuben Street where some members of the Jackson Hollow gang stood and watched. The heat was dangerously intense with two musicians and two policemen falling ill to the heat.[50]

Hugh Conroy, the man who had assisted Officer Scott into the drug store after the assault, had his own problems. John Ennis, a noteworthy South Brooklyn rough came to Grand Avenue and was arrested for assaulting Conroy because Conroy was not "friendly" to the Jackson Hollow Gang in his testimony.[51]

Ennis wasn't the last thug to go after Conroy. John McFadden approached Conroy on the street and told him that one of the gang members in jail named McCann would be released soon. Conroy said he replied that McCann was of no concern to him to which McFadden responded, "You son of a bitch. It was you who gave him away."

Conroy vigorously denied giving any testimony that implicated McCann, but McFadden attacked him. The two men fought in the street, but McFadden retreated when Conroy got the better of him. Conroy said he has been hounded by the Jackson Hollow Gang and that they have threatened to "lay him out."[52]

Hugh Conroy's assistance to Captain Leich in identifying the assailants of Officer Scott as well as the personal danger he placed himself in did not go unrewarded. The Commissioners appointed him a special policeman in order that he may have the protection of a shield.

All of the Jackson Hollow Gang arrested after Scott's murder were kept in jail while the police attempted to determine who actually threw the fatal stone. Captain Leich theorized it was James Whalehan who threw the stone, so the police investigation was slanted toward the Captain's belief. Even when detectives hinted that the Captain's theory may be wrong, Leich preferred to use his own judgement. If not for a message received by Justice Thomas Riley, the case might never have been solved. Riley was the judge who remanded the gang members to jail while the investigation continued. A friend of James Hurley, one of the jailed gang members, reached out to Riley and said Hurley wished to confess to him. When Hurley was brought into a private meeting with Riley, he was hesitant to talk to the judge, but eventually opened up. Hurley said that on the day of the murder he had been drinking heavily during the afternoon and evening and was very drunk. During the evening he was walking along Myrtle Avenue toward Steuben Street when he saw a crowd gathered at the corner. He said he heard someone cursing and saying that they will keep possession of the corner. Riley asked who had made the statement, but Hurley said he didn't know. Hurley continued to say that when he saw the boys were being ordered off by the policeman, he picked up a stone and threw it at him. Hurley saw the stone strike the policeman in the head, causing him to stagger and fall. Hurley said he didn't see anything after that and that he quickly got out of the area with the rest of the boys. Hurley said that he knew Scott and that it was not his intention to hurt him badly when he threw the stone. Hurley went on to say that he was finished with the Jackson Hollow Gang and that he would never drink again. Captain Leich was surprised and annoyed when he learned of Hurley's confession and realized his pet theory had been suddenly demolished.[53]

At the trial in a courtroom filled with young roughs, John Hurley was convicted of manslaughter in the third degree. At sentencing, Judge Henry Moore said the jury should have found Hurley guilty of murder but that all he could sentence Hurley to for the manslaughter verdict was four years in prison. Moore said the verdict was ludicrous because Hurley would have received a harsher sentence if he had broken into Officer Scott's house and robbed $50.00. Hurley showed no emotion during the sentencing.[54]

The Scott murder was the final straw for the Jackson Hollow Gang. From that point forward the gang received no mercy from the police. Gang members were arrested for even the pettiest offenses and received the maximum sentences allowed by statute. Slowly but surely the gang faded away.[55]

FEELING THE HEAT FROM THE HEAT

Another Brooklyn Policeman died a few days after officer Scott, but there was no manhunt required for his killer. It was well known that Officer Michael Colohon was slain by the extreme heat. 28-year-old Michael William Colohon was born in the Parish of Clurkented in County Galway, Ireland, and had been on the Brooklyn force for five years.[56]

During mid-July of 1876 Brooklynites were sweating through a severe heatwave. Numerous complaints were made by members of the Brooklyn Police force regarding the extraordinary heat and fatigue to which the men were being subjected. With the funerals of Police Commissioner Daniel Briggs and Officer Edward Scott only a couple of days apart, a protest was made against the inhumanity of compelling the men to march long distances on burning cobblestones with the thermometer at 104-degreees in the shade. Various precinct captains said that regardless of how important police funeral processions were, the health of the men would be severely impaired by making them march in the extreme heat.

George A. Waddy became a member of the police force of the city of Brooklyn in January 1851.[57] In 1876, at the rank of Inspector, Waddy was responsible for coordinating the activities at the funerals of Officer Scott and Commissioner Briggs. Waddy gave an order that all off duty officers were required to appear for the line of march. When asked about the danger from the heat Inspector Waddy laughed and said, "What are policemen made for if they cannot stand a little fatigue?"

The "little fatigue" caused over a dozen men to fall sick with sunstroke during the two marches. The torture of the march was doubly increased by the uniform the men were ordered to wear consisting of heavy dress coats buttoned to the chin, winter hats, belts, and clubs. With this heavy uniform, by the end of the march most men were as wet as though they had taken baths with their clothes on. While Inspector Waddy characterized the march as slightly fatiguing, he was careful to travel the entire distance of the march himself in a carriage.

Policeman Michael Colohan did not have a carriage to ride in. Colohon went on duty at 6 AM Friday morning. It was his "long day," when he had to work 18-hours out of 24-hours. He remained on duty until 6 PM, went home, had supper, and reported again for duty at midnight, when he again went on patrol and remained out until 6 AM on Saturday morning. The day and night had been oppressively hot, and Colohon was hardly able to stand. By Inspector Waddy's order, however, he was compelled to report for duty again at 8 AM, having only two hours in which to eat breakfast and recover from the fatigue of the previous 18-hours. Colohon did not complain and reported to the station house at 8 AM. He completed the funeral march for Commissioner Briggs and returned to the station house at 1 PM, rested until 6 PM, when he again reported for duty. His post was in the neighborhood of Smith and Butler Streets. During the evening he arrested John Clinton and Peter Barnett, two notorious young ruffians, the former for corner loafing and the latter for assault and battery. When he transported the prisoners to court, several officers made comments about his fatigued appearance, but Colohon just laughed and said that a few hours' sleep would set him straight. While in court, however, he showed signs of giving way, and was unable to sign the complaints against Clinton and Barnett.

Colohon approached court officer Connors and said, "I wish you would sign these complaints for me. I don't think I am able to."

"What's the matter with you Mike," Connors asked.

"Oh, I don't feel particularly bright," Colohon replied. "I have got terrible pains in my feet and across my back. I don't know what is the matter with me."

Connors signed the paperwork and advised Colohon to report sick. "I was just thinking about that," replied Colohon.

Colohon returned to the station house and was excused as sick by Sergeant Kellet who gave him a card for Police Surgeon Kissam, asking Kissam to examine Colohon. Instead of going to the doctor, however, Colohon went home and laid down, remaining in bed all day. At 2 PM on the next afternoon Colohon's wife woke him to ask if he was well enough to go to a christening on Butler Street. Colohon told his wife to go without him but that if he was feeling better, he would join her at 5 PM. His wife waited at the christening until 5 PM but Colohon did not arrive. At 6 PM his wife felt as if there may be a problem, so she returned home and found her husband lying in a semi-conscious condition on the bed, speechless and gasping for breath. She immediately sent for a doctor who arrived twenty minutes later. But it was too late, as Colohon had already passed away.[58]

Inspector Waddy was harshly criticized for compelling officers to march a great distance in the broiling sun, and in particular for the death of officer Colohon.[59] He continued in various positions until April 1, 1882, when he was retired on half pay, but he died shortly after his retirement.[60]

Twenty-two years later the heat may have played a roll in the death of another Brooklyn officer. As of July, 1898, Edward Loftus was leading the ordinary life of a policeman. He was appointed to the Brooklyn Police Department in 1890 and had recently become part of the Greater New York City Police Department after the consolidation. His record was good, and he lived with his wife and two children in Greenpoint.

All the normalcy came to an abrupt end on the evening of July 19th, 1898 when Patrolman Loftus appeared at the station house desk. Instead of proceeding to his post Loftus addressed the desk sergeant in civilian clothes and explained that he was resigning from the department because he had just inherited one million dollars. He then placed his shield and keys on the desk and departed the station house.[61] Two nights later Roundsman Vance and Patrolman Malley responded to investigate a large crowd at the corner of Greenpoint Avenue and Manhattan Avenue. The officers found that Edward Loftus was in the center of the crowd, singing popular songs and passing around his derby hat for pennies.

Vance and Malley took Loftus into custody but did not recognize him as a member of the police department. Sergeant Montague, the desk officer, did recognize Loftus and summoned Police Surgeon Charles Terry. Dr. Terry examined Loftus and determined he was mentally unbalanced. He was subsequently taken to Flatbush Hospital for a more thorough examination.[62]

The police investigation determined that after Loftus turned in his shield and keys the "demented" officer (that is the term used in the news article) had been roaming around Long Island City soliciting money, which he said was for a widows' and orphans' fund for the families of the men of the Seventy-First Regiment who were killed at the Battle of Santiago, a decisive naval engagement that occurred on July, 3, 1898, during the Spanish American War.[63]

Police colleagues and family said that Loftus was a well man up until a parade of city police on June 1st. Loftus marched in the parade from the Battery to 15th Street and then to 14th Street where the parade was dismissed. The day was hot, and the sun shone with uninterrupted brilliancy. On returning home, Loftus said he felt very tired. He could not eat anything and was unable to sleep that night, claiming that his head bothered him. He was never the same again, and in the opinion of his family, over-exertion in the heat during that parade caused him to lose his mind. His wife commented that several other officers dropped during the parade and had to be carried away in an ambulance.

Tragically, Edward Loftus never left Flatbush Hospital. He died on November 4th, 1900, after spending more than a year at the institution. In the news story detailing the 35-year old's death, the story of the circumstances leading up to his demise is quite different than previously detailed. This final story identifies the strike of the employees of the Brooklyn Heights Railroad Company as the main contributor to the officer's death. The article details how Loftus was compelled to perform extra duty during the strike, and that this overtaxing may have led to his dementia, as he began acting strangely after the strike duty. The article further notes that Loftus was retired on a half pay pension prior to his death.[64]

1890 PROFILE OF DEPARTMENT COMMAND STAFF

What a difference fourteen years makes. In 1876 the Eagle's profile of the members of Brooklyn's Fourth Precinct was filled with biting, cutting, and sarcastic remarks about the competence and characteristics of the officers assigned to the precinct. In 1890, however, the Eagle described the Brooklyn Police Department as the equal to any police force in the nation. It noted how the department had evolved from the half deaf, half blind and generally decrepit old watchmen of the village days, with his cumbrous rattle and still more cumbrous "Upper Benjamin," to the tall, straight and athletic young fellow of 1890. By the way, I believe an "Upper Benjamin" was some type of overcoat.

At times, the numerical strength of the department did not keep up with Brooklyn's growth, but the quality of the police officers had improved greatly. In 1890 the utmost care was exercised in the selection of recruits, with each applicant being compelled to undergo a thorough physical and general knowledge examination. "If a "black sheep" did manage to creep through, it would not be long before the disciplinary process would catch up with the miscreant and lead to dismissal from the force. According to the eagle the department was never as well organized as it was in 1890 with those in authority having in every instance worked their way up the ranks through merit.

In 1890 the muster roll of the department showed 1,255 men, along with the superintendent and three inspectors. There were 19-captains, 80-sergeants, 46-detective sergeants, 38- roundsmen, 40-doormen, 20-bridgekeepers, 12-telegraph and linemen, and 1,000 patrolmen.

Police pay was good although there was always some agitating for an increase, and the department had no trouble finding recruits. Some veteran officers looked down on those designated as "Civil Service men," having been hired after the new civil service reforms.

One of the big advances in efficiency in 1890 was the introduction of the patrol wagon system. When an officer made an arrest, they no longer had to escort the prisoner to the station house in person, leaving his post uncovered for an hour or more. With the patrol wagon system, the arresting officer went to the nearest patrol box to send a signal to his station requesting the patrol wagon.

In 1890 the head of the Brooklyn Police Department was Henry L. Hayden. Hayden was a member of an old Connecticut family and a native of New Haven.
His father was chief of police of New Haven for a number of years, and Mr. Hayden served under his father as a clerk for five years. Early in the Civil War Hayden received a life appointment in the Navy from President Lincoln and served on the sloop of war Portsmouth, which was attached to Admiral Farragaut's fleet. He was present at the capture of New Orleans and took part in other engagements, resigning his position at the end of the war and taking up residence in Brooklyn.

Henry L. Hayden

The Eagle points out that Mr. Hayden was a Democrat, but that before he was appointed to the position of Parks Commissioner in July 1889, his name was seldom mentioned in connection with politics. His appointment as Police Commissioner was a great surprise to the rank and file of the party and probably to himself as well. He was respected and liked by his subordinates and enjoyed the confidence of the public to the fullest degree.

Suavity, kindness, and the ability to get through almost any amount of work were the principle characteristics of Deputy Police Commissioner Francis L. Dallon. Although not born in Brooklyn Mr. Dallon spent his entire business life and political career in the city. In 1850 he studied law in the office of Crook & Campbell, and in July 1855, he was admitted to the bar. When he assumed the position of Deputy Police Commissioner Mr. Dallon was 60-years old, but still hale, hearty and unafraid of work. He was a lover of music and books and was fond of all forms of quiet amusement.

Francis L. Dallon

Superintendent Campbell was born in 1827 in the city of Charleston, South Carolina, but when he was quite young his parents moved to Brooklyn. He secured employment in the office of the Brooklyn Daily Eagle, beginning at the bottom of the ladder. He worked his way up to become the foreman of the Eagle composing room. Very early in life he began to take interest in politics. He became a man of influence and during the administration of President Pierce his services were rewarded by an appointment as Inspector of Customs. In 1866 he was elected by the democratic party Sheriff of Kings County. In 1870 Brooklyn adopted the Metropolitan System for its police force and Campbell was made Chief of Police. A change in the city charter abolished the office, and on August 12, 1875, he was appointed Superintendent of Police. From the first hour he assumed command of the force he was animated by one idea – efficiency within the department. Before his administration, Brooklyn was infested with gangs and thieves, many who made regular raids from New York. As the executive head of the department the superintendent did much toward increasing the efficiency of the detective corps. There were many men with more detective ability than Campbell, but none with more dogged perseverance.

Superintendent Campbell

Inspector Mackellar, the senior inspector of the department was born in New York City in 1842, and his parents moved to Brooklyn in 1845. The Inspector did not go to war, but he found plenty of fighting closer to home. In July 1863, Mackellar enlisted in the special force organized to put down the draft riots in New York City. He was on duty day and night during the week of the rioting and received his fair share of hard knocks. When the trouble was over, he was transferred to the Atlantic Dock Squad, a body of men organized to protect property and storehouses in South Brooklyn. In June 1864 Mackellar was made a regular patrolman and six months later he was promoted to sergeant. In 1872 he was promoted to captain and ten years later he was advanced to the rank of inspector. Inspector Mackellar was thoughtful and rather retiring, but he could also be very entertaining. He took the place of the superintendent when the latter was absent. Inspector Mackellar also supervised the instruction of recruits, grounding them in the duties of good policemen and supplementing his teachings with solid and fatherly advice.

Inspector Mackellar

Inspector Edward Reilly was born in New York City in 1842, but lived in Brooklyn for almost his entire life. During the Civil War he enlisted in Company G of the Ninth New York Volunteers. He was in the engagement at Big Bethel and took part in the capture of Fort Hatteras and Fort Clarke. On June 3, 1867, he joined the Brooklyn Police Department as a patrolman, and in 1870 he was promoted to sergeant. In 1875 Reilly was promoted to captain, and in 1880 he was advanced to inspector. In 1887 Reilly was head of the detective branch of the service.

Inspector Edward Reilly

Inspector Patrick McGlaughlin was born in Brooklyn in1842. In 1861 he enlisted as a private in the 173rd Regiment of the New York Volunteers. He served under General Sheridan for three years, being cited for bravery several times and earning a promotion to first lieutenant. At the conclusion of the Civil War McGlaughlin returned to Brooklyn and in 1866 he was appointed to the Brooklyn Police Department. He quickly rose through the ranks and as a captain he served as commanding officer of the Eighth and Ninth Precincts until being elevated to the rank of inspector. Along with his other duties McGlaughlin acted as the department drill instructor, a position he was imminently qualified for due to his experience and study of military tactics.[65]

Inspector Patrick McGlaughlin

THE DEATH OF OFFICER JOHN DONAHOE

The most important event of 1872 was the murder of Patrolman John Donahoe, of the Fifth Precinct, on the night of July 7th, by Henry Rodgers. Donahoe left the station house shortly after midnight to begin his patrol. On his post was the Crow's Gin Mill, a saloon with an unsavory reputation. Donahoe had made several arrests at the establishment and was aware that many of the bar's patrons held a grudge against him, some even vowing to "lay the officer out." On several occasions some of the local toughs laid in wait for the officer, but the presence of strangers or other police in the area scared them off. On this night, however, thirteen of the gang assembled in front of the saloon, with Rodgers leading the group and holding a heavy cart-rung.

The Crow was located in a section known as Battle Row and was a dilapidated, one-story, low-class saloon that was a favorite hangout of the Battle Row Gang.

When Donahoe approached the area, the Crow was closed, but about a dozen of the Battle Row Gang were congregated outside the saloon. They were all drunk and Henry Rodgers had already armed himself with a heavy club fashioned from a cart-rung, muttering thirty minutes earlier that he intended to "lay Donahoe out."

When the gang observed Donahoe approaching they began singing loud drunken choruses of "Down in the Coal Mine," and "Heave Away, My Hearty." Donahoe ordered the group to cease the singing which was causing a disturbance to the surrounding neighborhood. When the policeman turned to walk away Rodgers came up from behind and struck him as hard as he could on the head with his club. Donahoe fell to the sidewalk, but Rodgers continued beating him with the club until it broke into two pieces.[66]

A German man who lived in the tenement next to the saloon looked out his window and saw the officer lying on the sidewalk. He ran to Donahoe and raised an alarm, bringing several people to the scene, including Policemen Cantwell and Travers, who were patrolling the adjoining posts. The officers lifted Donahoe onto a cart, and with the assistance of several citizens, pulled the cart back to the station house. It was ironic that Henry Rodgers had returned to the scene and was actually one of the citizens helping to pull the cart.

At the station house, Police Surgeon Brady attended to Officer Donahoe, but he also noticed the jittery nature of Rodgers. Brady also noticed a dark blood stain on Rodgers' vest, and when he inquired about it, Rodgers became very nervous and quickly left the station house. Brady went to Sergeant Bunce, the station house desk officer, and told him that he believed Rodgers was the culprit who had struck Officer Donahoe. Sergeant Bunce directed Officer Holland to find Rodgers, and within an hour Rodgers was in custody. Officer Donahoe was transported to the City Hospital where he died a few days later.

John Donahue was born in 1840 in the County of Cavan, in Ireland. He emigrated to the United States at the age of eleven and took up residence in Williamsburg. He was sent to school for a while and after receiving an ordinary amount of education, he began learning the trade of brass-finisher. When the Civil War began, he served three years in the Navy and participated under Admiral Farragaut in the Battle of New Orleans and the surrender of Charleston. At the conclusion of his military service

Donahue returned to Brooklyn and became a member of the Metropolitan Police Force. Donahue was married with two children. He was 5 feet 7 inches tall, powerfully built, with a fair complexion and dark brown hair and moustache. For two years he was a member of the same volunteer fire engine company to which Rodgers also belonged.

Henry Rodgers stood trial for murder and was found guilty after the jury deliberated for four hours. Presiding Judge Jasper W. Gilbert sentenced Rodgers to hang. During the trial Rodgers never denied striking Donohue, and his only defense was alleging that fellow gang member John Denver had told him to hit the officer.

Rodgers did not sleep more than a few moments the night before his execution. Two Catholic priests, Father McDonald and Father McElroy stayed with the condemned man in the time leading up to the execution. At 6 AM Rodgers was given a breakfast of a cup of tea and a plate of toast. He sipped some of the tea but left the toast untouched. He then leisurely washed and dressed before a barber arrived at 6:30 and shaved him.

At 8 AM a contingent of police officers marched into the jail yard and took positions around the gallows. At this same time the writ of execution was read to Rodgers in his cell. The doomed man listened to the reading without exhibiting any emotion. He then said a final farewell to several prison officials.

At 9 AM about five hundred spectators had gathered in the prison yard. At 9:35 Rodgers was taken from his cell. Rodgers made his way to the gallows supported on either side by Father McDonald and Father McElroy. When Rodgers was about six feet from the dangling rope, Father McDonald read the Services for the Dead. Rodgers held Father McElroy's arm tightly. In his left hand he held rosary beads and in his right hand a crucifix which he kissed. He was dressed in a fine suit, clean shirt, and a shiny black necktie. His chin was cleanly shaven, and his hair neatly brushed back behind the ears, and his moustache and whiskers smoothed and trimmed. As Father McDonald prayed Rodgers drooped and looked as if he was about to faint. He would have fallen to the ground if not supported by Father McElroy. Rodgers revived in about thirty seconds and was led under the rope. The hangman pulled the hood over Rodgers' face and adjusted the noose. When the signal was given to the hangman a dull thud sounded and Rodgers was lifted to a height of about six feet. He hung from the rope for nineteen minutes until being brought down and pronounced dead.

Thirty-year-old Henry Rodgers was born in Brooklyn. Very early in life he began hanging around on the streets with an assortment of unsavory characters. He usually spent his night in low class saloons in Williamsburg and before reaching the age of twenty he was recognized as being a leading member of the Battle Row Gang. Rodgers had a long criminal history, but his political affiliations and the fear of the Battle Row Gang had shielded him from any significant punishment. During the last stages of the Civil War Rodgers served two years in the Fifth New York Artillery. He was always regarded with distrust by his fellow soldiers – a coward when sober and a most treacherous man when drunk. When his military service was complete, Rodgers returned to Williamsburg and obtained a job in a blacksmith's shop in the navy yard, but he was only able to hold the job for a short period of time. Rodgers was unmarried but at the time of his execution he was engaged to a dressmaker who had been a constant visitor while he was incarcerated. Rodgers' mother, although living in Williamsburg, did not know her son was in trouble until he was condemned to die. After he was sentenced Rodgers had many visits from his mother, whose whereabouts she was unaware of, even though they both lived in the same neighborhood.[67]

The Battle Row Gang – This gang, which had an almost two-decade-long life starting in 1870, was in the words of the Brooklyn Daily Eagle "composed of the scum of the Fourteenth Ward (Williamsburg)." Known as "fighters and rowdies," they lurked at "Crow," McGoldrick's saloon on Union Avenue and North First Street. After Rodgers killed officer Donahoe, two factions of the gang fought with pistols, knives, fists and slingshots. The battle raged, furiously and unrestrained for thirty minutes. One dying member, Patrick Cash, asked to name his assailants replied, "I'd die with the name of the fellow in my throat, before I'd give him away."[68]

DETECTIVES

In 1887 the detectives of the Brooklyn Police Department were broken into two groups. Thirty-five detectives were spread amongst the precincts while nine were assigned to the Central Office. Throughout the latter half of the 19th century the detective function had increased, both in size and skill. The reasons for these advancements were rooted in the fact that crime had become more and more scientific over time and criminals more sophisticated. The typical criminals of the era were intelligent and educated, with the skills necessary to be successful in the professional and business circles of society. Unfortunately, their talents were prostituted for illegal uses.

To prevent criminal successes, as well as to capture the offenders, the quality of the detectives had to be advanced. The detective had to possess a mind superior to that of his antagonist. He had to be endowed with a clear, honest and comprehensive understanding which enabled him to fathom the depths of criminal science, and a force of will and vigor of body that was necessary to overcome the nature and the disposition of the men with whom he had to contend.

Some of the best detectives on the police department were assigned to the Central Office and are profiled below.

William D. Strong was a son of the Hon. Demas Strong, one of the best-known citizens of the Eastern District, where he was born in 1845. In September 1873, at the age of twenty-eight, he joined the force and did duty as patrolman. In 1885 he was appointed to the detective corps. In 1887 Mr. Strong was in charge of the Rogues Gallery, as well as the clerical portion of the work in the detective department. He kept a record of each criminal photographed, his pedigree in crime, physical peculiarities and distinguishing marks. Neat and careful in his attire, Strong was in great demand at great balls, receptions and parties. When attired in evening costume he was indistinguishable from the guests. A part of his work was patrolling the thoroughfares which were crowded with shoppers. Here his invaluable knowledge of pickpockets and sneak thieves, blackmailers and crooks was put into constant use, and served to save the public from depredations of all sorts.

Detective Michael F. Powers was a thick-set muscular man about forty-two years of age in 1887. After some years of service on the New York police force, he became a patrolman on the Brooklyn force in the spring of 1870. On July 26th of the same year, he received his detective appointment. Powers was connected with many celebrated cases, and it was notable that most of the criminals he arrested were convicted.

Detective Jas. H. Roche was 41-years old in 1887. He became a patrolman May 12th,1869, and was promoted to the rank of detective in July,1871, where he continually served either on Precinct or Central Office duty. In connection with his associates he had closed the policy shops of Brooklyn, which at one time were a crying evil.

Patrick Corr was the senior in service of the Central Office Detective Squad in 1887. He was fifty-two years of age and had been on the force since January 13, 1857. He performed patrol duty until the spring of 1869 when he was assigned to the Fourth Precinct as detective. In 1874 he was transferred to the Central Office. Discreet, close-mouthed, indefatigable and intelligent, he earned a reputation that would do honor to the best of men. He had a large acquaintanceship among the "confidence men" of Brooklyn and New York City. He told many good stories of their tricks and wiles, but none superior to the following:

"I was strolling downtown the other morning, and feeling hungry, dropped into a restaurant. There, large as life, was a boss crook whom I have taken in once or twice, but who generally succeeds in evading or escaping the law. I sat down at the same table and asked him what he was doing now."

He smiled, winked and replied: "I have found honesty to be the best policy, and have gone into a legitimate business."

"What is that?" I asked, having missed him from his usual haunts.

"Teaching the innocent rustic and unsophisticated suburban. I average one scholar a day, and the scheme pays very well. I struck the racket last winter and have found it a picnic."

"How do you work it?"

"I put a card in fifty country newspapers: *'Fortunes Made. Gamblers Tricks Exposed. Marked Cards, Loaded Dice, Bugs and Patent Boxes for sale, with instructions. Lessons at Reasonable Rates. Address 222.'* The rustic sees this, and in the same paper reads of a man winning $25,000 at Faro. He writes me and I send him a price list. It is the same as that used by regular dealers in gambling goods, only about fifty per cent higher in prices. If the fellow wants to buy, I sell and make a decent profit. But what catches is a notice at the end - *Having been a professional gambler twenty years, I am familiar with every trick of the trade, and guarantee to make any novice proficient in three lessons, and skillful enough to meet any blackleg on equal terms. Terms, $ 1 a lesson of one hour.* The chump reads that and comes on and calls. I have a deal with the landlord of the place I board at and receive my pupil in the parlor. The best racket is to teach him to use loaded dice or marked cards. In an hour he's got the hang of it; but of course, he is very clumsy. We go down to the nearest barroom and throw for drinks. My pal comes up to the bar and looks interested in the game, and asks us to let him in. I say 'certainly' and give my bucolic friend the wink. My pal then loses two or three rounds and wants to throw for a quarter a head. We accede. My pal loses, the rustic beats him, but I win. After a few throws I pull my watch out and plead an engagement and get out. As I leave, I whisper to the countryman that he has a picnic, and to work the fellow for all he is worth. I then skip. The game continues, and in fifteen minutes my pupil is cleaned out. If he kicks my pal suddenly picks up one of the loaded dice and starts a row. If the man isn't a fighter, my pal hits him on the nose. If he is, we call on the gang that hangs around all saloons and bounce him for a blackleg. You can bet he never comes back, and he doesn't complain to the police. Even if he did, we'd have the dead wood on him and could easily prove that he rung in loaded dice on us. The racket's just the same with marked cards, but only a little slower. What do you think of the game? "

"Ingenious; but doesn't the landlord of the boarding house, or the saloon object?"

"No! Don't you see we divvy up? According to how good the business is, we yield from 15 to 10 per cent. Why, I'd give 70 per cent if I could work a first class hotel. On the proceeds I and my pal go halves. How much do we collar? Can't say. Anywhere from an X up. Old Long Island farmers and New Jersey deacons generally come to town quite well fixed, and they often yield a century. The funniest thing in the whole matter is that the rustic never tumbles to me. Three or four times I've met suckers we'd worked, and every time they came up, shook hands and treated. They'd tell me yarns how they put up jobs with the tricks I taught them, but they never spoke of their losses."

John E. Lowery was born in 1857. In 1878 he entered the ranks as a patrolman, and for seven years did good service in that capacity. In 1880 he was made a detective but had only been attached to the Central Office since January 1887. Lowery was very good- natured and very popular.

Detective Edward Looney was a man forty years of age in 1887. He was appointed to the force in 1870 and served for a year as patrolman. In 1871 he was made roundsman, and in 1873, sergeant. In 1875 he assumed his present position on the Central Office Squad. A man of great bravery, he had time and again, when duty demanded it, risked his life when death seemed inevitable. Looney was regarded as an authority upon burglars and burglaries by his associates. He had more experience with this class of criminals than most officials of the land. His description of the Knight of the Jimmy is worth repeating.

"There are fashions in the way of committing burglaries just as there are in bonnets. The really first-class workmen, who undertake nothing but gigantic jobs, are generally English. Some men tackle nothing but banks and stores, making the opening of a safe a specialty. Dwelling- house robbery is falling into disrepute in the big cities but is still in vogue in the country. Many of the most useful operators do nothing but plan. When they have made the line of attack out, as they would prospect the moves in a game of chess, they pass the scheme over to the workers. Burglars' tools are always constructed of the finest materials. Some of them illustrate the application of deeper principles of natural philosophy than we ever imagined in an honest workshop, and there are iron and steel contrivances, used in opening safes, the nature and purposes of which would utterly confound a safe manufacturer. The hour selected is generally about 3 AM, the chances being in favor of the inmates having all encamped in the pleasant land of dreams. A back shutter is pried open; a balcony is scaled, and a second story window raised; or they may go through the coal hole in the pavement and force the door at the kitchen stairs. Sometimes the job is done alone, and then again there are several engaged, one remaining outside as a sentinel. A burglar in alluding to the attempt to rob a tailor's store in Washington Street, which resulted in the arrest of two young men who have since been sentenced to five years each in prison, said it was all the fault of the lookout. A 'lookout' occupies a very responsible position, whether on board a ship or connected with a burglary. Imagine the burglar in the house. He has reached the parlor floor and pauses to listen. The darkness, the silence, must be terrible. His own breathing seems like a mighty storm of wind. Satisfied that there is no one in the immediate neighborhood, he produces his lantern. Cautiously, and in a second, as he sweeps it about, gets the lay of the land. If he is after plate, the dining-room is visited, the pantry and butler's closet forced, and the articles of silverware piled high upon the table, ready to be done up in the tablecloth, or thrust into a less suspicious bag provided for the purpose."

Detective John Rall was appointed a policeman January 21, 1872, and after a number of years became a detective, and was detailed as a member of the Central Office Squad. He was a very silent man and was not as well-known as his colleagues. He had done much good work and was in every way a trustworthy man. He was conversant with all the ways of criminals.

"Crooks have one queer feature," he said, "and that is they like to describe and exaggerate their exploits to their legal enemies—the police. I presume every officer can relate a dozen good stories thus told him by some malefactor."

One of the more skilled and notable detectives on the Brooklyn Police force was George V. Zundt. He was forty-two years of age in 1887, had a dark complexion, was rather stout, and was very intelligent and interesting. At the age of fifteen, he enlisted in the Thirteenth Regiment New York Volunteers, and fought in the Civil War. He served three months and upon his return he re-entered in the ranks of the Thirteenth and served another month. He then enlisted in the Fifty-Fourth New York

Volunteers and fought until the war was over. Zundt became a patrolman February 6th, 1871, and served in that capacity until 1875,when he was appointed a detective, and detailed to the Central Office. His experiences with malefactors were extremely varied, including almost every form of crime.

Superintendent Campbell was strongly in favor of Zundt's selection as detective because of his shrewdness and his knowledge of the German language, a skill possessed by no other detective.

The robbery of John Connors was the first big case Zundt grappled with, and his brilliant management of the case brought him into prominence. Two gold watches of considerable value and $1,500 in cash had been stolen from Connors. The robbery was apparently the work of a sneak thief who was familiar with the Smith Street house and Connor's habits. Two or three of the veteran detectives at headquarters were baffled by the crime and theorized that possibly no crime at all had taken place.

Zundt commenced his investigation and quickly focused on a girl who had worked as a domestic for one of Connor's relatives more than a year earlier. What interested Zundt was the fact that Connors had stayed at the relative's home for a period of time while the girl was employed there. Connors said he had forgotten about the girl and scoffed at the detective's suspicions because he said the girl did not know the location of his home. Zundt felt he was on the right track, however, because a girl fitting his suspect's description was known to hang out at night in the neighborhood of Connors' home. Zundt was eventually able to track the girl to her mother's home in Bushwick. While maintaining a surveillance on the mother's house Zundt observed the girl coming out of the door. He walked up to her and said, "How are you, Miss Annie Cody?"

"You are mistaken," was the girls curt response.

"I guess not," Zundt shot back. "I believe Mrs. Cody lives upstairs and that you are her daughter; at all events I will go up and see and will ask you to favor me with your company."

The young woman at first refused, but eventually consented to accompany Detective Zundt into her home. Upon entering the house, before the girl could say anything, Zundt quickly asked, "Is this your daughter?"

The woman inside the house responded, "She is."

Zundt told the girl, who now admitted she was Annie Cody, that he wanted her to accompany him to police headquarters. Annie broke down crying that her sister was in the next room lying near death. Zundt looked into the room and was surprised to see a doctor attending to a bedridden woman. The detective still insisted that Annie accompany him, and she consented, but asked that she be allowed to say a final goodbye to her sister in private. Detective Zundt allowed the farewell but insisted on being inside the room with Annie. When Annie leaned over her sister Zundt observed her take something out of her pocket and place it under the sick woman's clothes. The items Annie was trying to hide turned out to be two pawn tickets for watches that had been stolen from Connors. With the discovery of this irrefutable evidence, Annie made a full confession to Detective Zundt. She explained how she would quietly enter the house where Connors lived and hide in the closet in his bedroom. She said she remained hidden in the closet until Connors was asleep at which time she would come out from hiding and go through Connors pockets and the rest of the house, leaving with various cash and property. Annie was subsequently tried and convicted and sentenced to a year in prison.

Detective Zundt had, among other wrong doers, arrested many blackmailers. One case was quite out of the ordinary as Zundt explained.

"A short time ago I was called on professionally by a gentleman who wished my aid in getting rid of a man and woman who had pestered him grievously. He had met them at one of the fashionable hotels at the Catskills, and had carried on a flirtation with the woman, who was young and fascinating. Of course, he had compromised himself; and the result was that he had been visited unexpectedly by the woman's alleged husband, who demanded, under pain of the fullest exposure, $10,000. He gave the man his check for $ 7,000 on one of the city banks, thinking that was the easiest way to settle the trouble, and was assured that there the matter would rest. A month later he received a letter, in which an additional sum of money was demanded. Realizing that compliance with this request would render him liable to further assessments, he placed the matter in my hands. I saw at once that he had been the victim of blackmailers and immediately called on the outraged husband, who had come down from Garrisons that day, and was then waiting to meet my patron at a neighboring saloon. He grew highly indignant when I informed him that he would not get another dollar and threatened to lick me when I told him I would send him to State Prison if he further annoyed the gentleman. I gave him a good choking and, I think, discolored his eyes when he became unbearably insolent, which so frightened the villain that he has not been heard of since."[69]

Martin Segellesen walked wearily through the rows of corn stalks. Every day the scene in the field was identical since he began working on Deidrich Wessel's East New York farm. On this day, however, something out of the ordinary caught his eye. A woman's shawl lay next to a tall stalk. As he approached the shawl Martin recoiled in horror when he observed a woman's body lying next to the shawl. So, began Detective George Zundt's greatest case.

A pictorial summary of the Sarah Alexander murder case

Detective Zundt methodically pieced together the evidence in the case. The victim was identified as Sarah Alexander, and a bloody knife was found near thebody. The post-mortem examination of the body revealed that the victim was pregnant at the time of her death.

Sarah Alexander lived with her family in New York City very close to relatives, the Rubenstein family. Sarah was very close to her cousin, Pasach Rubenstein. Detective Zundt's investigation found several witnesses who identified Pasach Rubenstein and Sarah Alexander as being on the same streetcar together, with both getting off the car in the vicinity of the East New York corn field.

That was enough evidence for Inspector Waddy to direct Zundt to the Rubenstein home at 83 Bayard Street to arrest Pasach Rubenstein. The address where the Rubenstein's resided was also a combined dry goods and jewelry store. Pasach's mother was in the store and said that her son was not there, but that she expected him back soon. Detective Zundt did not reveal the purpose of his visit, but instead focused on buying a pair of gloves. Zundt went through several pairs of gloves, finding each unsatisfactory, until Pasach Rubenstein entered the store. He ran in as though he was being pursued by someone, and only stopped when Detective Zundt called out to him. "Mr. Rubenstein, I want you to come to the morgue in Brooklyn. They have your cousin there and the coroner wants you to identify the body."

"My brothers and father can do it," Pasach replied.

"Well," Zundt said, "the coroner wants you – he wants several relatives to identify her before he gives the body up for burial."

"Oh, no, no," Pasach moaned. "I don't want to go – I don't want to go."

Then he ran into the back room and brought out a pair of earrings. "See," he said, "I gave that girl a pair like this."

"Yes," Zundt nodded, "She's wearing earrings like that, but I need you to come with me."

"Oh, no, no, no," Rubenstein repeated. "I don't want to go."

"Come on now," said Zundt, "or I'll take you by force." As he spoke Zundt grabbed Pasach by the collar and pushed him out of the store.

At the morgue, Detective Zundt led Rubenstein to the table containing the body.

"Do you know that girl?" the coroner asked.

"Yes," replied Pasach. He seemed to try to get as far away from the body as possible, but the coroner insisted that he take a closer look.

"Step around there," the coroner motioned to the right side of the slab. "You can't see the face where you are now. Have you seen that girl before?"

Pasach's face was more deathly looking than the girl on the slab. "Yes, I seen her, Yes, I seen her."

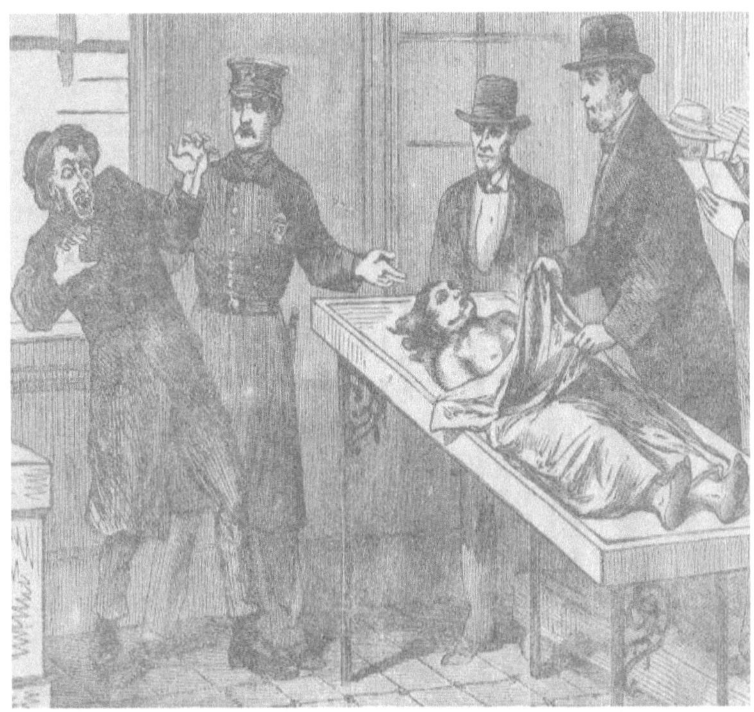

Pasach kept nodding his head but would move no closer to the body. The coroner beckoned Rubenstein to come closer and he reluctantly obeyed. Pasach inched closer to the body until the coroner grabbed him by the collar and made him step close to the slab. "You are sure you know this woman?" he said.

Pasach continued to nod as the coroner removed the shawl to reveal the head and wound in its entirety. "Look now!" the coroner directed.

Pasach let out a sharp quick cry of terror as he pulled himself free from the coroner's grasp, jumped backwards from the table, and threw up his hands as if to hide the body from his sight.

Detective Zundt took Rubenstein to police headquarters where he denied killing Sarah or being with her on the day of the murder. Zundt left Pasach in custody to interview his family members, and he received conflicting statements from Pasach's mother and sister as to his whereabouts during the day of the murder.

Detective Zundt established a potential motive for the crime when he learned that Pasach's wife was due to arrive in New York very soon. Zundt had learned from several interviews that Pasach had been in a secret, intimate relationship with Sarah, and that the baby she was carrying was his. Zundt theorized that Pasach lured Sarah to the cornfield with the promise of spending some intimate time together, when in reality, he chose the isolated location as the spot to get rid of his problem before his wife arrived. The theory made sense, but most of the evidence was circumstantial. Detective Zundt would need more hard evidence.

The first piece of hard evidence was obtained when Zundt got a storekeeper to identify the bloody knife found in the cornfield as the same knife he sold to Pasach Rubenstein. The second damning piece of evidence came when Officer Clifford was sent to the murder scene and lifted boot prints and smaller footprints from the field. The result was that Pasach's boots matched the larger footprints perfectly and the slain girl's shoes were a perfect match to the smaller footprints. So clear were these tracks that the break in one of the soles of Pasach's shoes was plainly visible.[70]

There were several reports of unsuccessful attempts of bribes on the part of the Rubenstein family to get Pasach released from jail and to get the shopkeeper to change her testimony regarding the fact that she had sold Pasach the bloody knife found at the scene of the crime.

Pasach Rubenstein stood trial for the murder of Sarah Alexander. When the jury pronounced him guilty, Rubenstein raised his hands, threw his head back, fixed his eyes on the judge and cried in a piercing tone, "I don't want to give up my blood."

The scene inside the courtroom was chaotic. Those in the gallery mounted seats and strained to see everything going on. Judge Moore brought the room to order and went forward with the sentencing. "Rubenstein, it is now the duty of the Court to pronounce on you its sentence for the crime of which you have been convicted. Your case has been patiently and carefully tried by a jury of peculiar intelligence. Your counsel have defended you with and ability and zeal which could not be surpassed, but they have labored in vain for you. The terrible, might I say providential, circumstances have been too overwhelming. I will not recapitulate the history of your crime. It is too horrible to contemplate. One, who had a right by ties of race, religion, and blood, to look to you for protection, was by an atrocious act enticed to a lonely spot and butchered without mercy. The law not only requires that you should be fairly tried, but it gives you time to prepare for death, which you brutally denied to your victim, Listen to the sentence of the Court which is: That you be taken to the jail from which you came, and on Friday, the 24th of March, between the hours of nine in the morning and two in the afternoon, you be hanged by the neck until you are dead, and may God have mercy on your soul."

At the conclusion of the sentencing, Rubenstein blurted, "I am not satisfied!"

Rubenstein's outburst in court

Rubenstein was placed in one of the "condemned cells" in the Raymond Street jail. These cells were reserved for prisoners awaiting execution.

While incarcerated, Rubenstein asked to see Detective Zundt and Pesach Alexander, the brother of the murdered girl. When the visitors were in the cell Rubenstein turned to Alexander and declared his innocence. He then turned toward Zundt and commenced making accusations and threats. "You have brought me to the gallows. I am a doomed man, and you are the sole cause of placing me in the position I am in now. My blood will be on you and will follow your wife and your children. You will suffer for this, it may not be this month or next month, but my blood shall follow you, and my kindred will not forget the thing you have done."

Detective Zundt said he was only doing his duty, but Rubenstein continued to shake with anger, "You have frightened my witnesses from coming over here to swear in my behalf, and you have threatened that they would be harmed if they dared to speak the truth of me."

Zundt again tried to explain that he was doing his duty, but Rubenstein would not hear of it, again repeating that the detective and his family would suffer, and that his blood would follow them until a terrible revenge had been obtained. Rubenstein went on to say that he wanted to make this declaration in front of the victim's brother and to declare his innocence.

Pasach Rubenstein never made it to the gallows. He died in his jail cell on May 4th, 1876, from causes directly brought about by lack of proper nourishment and the unhygienic environment of the cell. Some say Rubenstein, in effect, committed suicide. It was not certain that he deliberately adopted a course that would lead to his death, but he constantly refused to eat much of his food and had refused to wash himself. Added to this he observed long and rigid periods of fasting, which combined with his filthy surroundings, served to completely undermine his health.[71]

One needs to look no further than books, television, and movies to see American's fascination with "the big heist." This is especially true when the target of the crime is a bank. This phenomenon of the big heist was present in 19th century Brooklyn, drawing extensive newspaper coverage regardless of how ineptly the crime was committed.

The Brooklyn Bank was established in 1832 and was long considered one of the solid banking institutions in the city. Gilbert L. Whiting was a bookkeeper at the bank earning an annual salary of $2,200.00. A few days before the heist the bank directors held a meeting where it was decided that expenses would have to be cut, including employees' salaries. Whiting was informed that his salary was being reduced to $1,500.00.

The reduction in salary effected Whiting so much that he concocted a ridiculous plan to embezzle the bank's money. His plan was to take the money and then negotiate with the bank to return some of it. On the afternoon of his scheme while he was alone inside the bank for a short time, Whiting opened the vault with the combination he knew. He filled two valises with money before leaving the bank. Since he was the last person in the vault, he would get the ten-to-twelve-hour head start he figured he needed before the theft was discovered. He also left a letter inside the vault explaining his willingness to negotiate a return of some of the money and instructing the bank president to place the following personal ad in the Herald: "*W.LG. – We agree to your proposal – B.B.*"

The next morning the theft was discovered, and the police were notified. Superintendent Campbell considered the case so serious that he personally responded to the bank to begin the investigation. Campbell eventually returned to headquarters and summoned Detectives Corwin and Looney, instructing them to watch Whiting's home on Macon Street. The detectives proceeded to the home and had a conversation with Whiting's wife. She said she knew nothing of her husband's crime and gave the detectives a letter from her husband in which he said he had travelled to Baltimore. On the advice of Superintendent Campbell, bank officials published the aforementioned personal ad in the Herald. The message in the paper had the desired effect because at ten o'clock the next morning Gilbert Whiting very quietly entered his home and was promptly arrested.

While taking their prisoner to headquarters Whiting offered Corwin and Looney the contents of a valise he carried in his hand if they let him go. Inside the valise was

$125,320.62. The detectives refused the bribe and brought the perpetrator to headquarters where he was interviewed by the Superintendent. The embezzler informed the Superintendent that there was another valise containing more money at the Van Dyke House on the Bowery in New York City. The Superintendent immediately dispatched the detectives to the location where they found a valise containing $28,756.00. In total, $154,056.62 was recovered, which is the equivalent of $4.2 million today. In an era when politics, corruption, and payoffs were closely linked to police work, it was refreshing to see an instance where a life-changing bribe was rejected by two honest detectives.[72]

Corwin and looney subsequently received a $200 reward from the bank. The department took 10% of the reward for the Police Relief Fund.[73] Whiting was 42, married with three children. He was a prominent member of the Tompkins Avenue Congressional Church. He had worked at the bank for years, working his way up to his current position.[74]

Many were convinced Whiting was insane. They reasoned that only an insane person would take the bank's money, leave a note in the vault, and then think he would escape justice because a personal ad said they agreed to his proposal. To further the lunacy argument, it was thought that when Whiting was picked up by detectives stepping out of his house, he was on his way to the bank to negotiate with the president how much of the money he would have to return.[75]

Gilbert Whiting's plan for the heist may have been ridiculous, but at least he had a plan. Christian Berghauser illustrated the pitfalls of attempting a heist with no plan at all.

On January 3, 1878, 45-year-old Christian Berghauser frantically ran down Wythe Avenue being chased by a group of young boys. As he ran, Berghauser shouted, "Help me! The boys are trying to rob me. If someone gets me safely home, I will give them $500."

He ran into the fish market at 90 Wythe Avenue and nearly knocked over proprietor John Stucks. A crowd of boys gathered around the door to the store hooting and yelling while Berghauser cowered in the middle of the store attempting to catch his breath. The man held a hat that was filled with money against his chest, and he appealed to Stucks to help him get to his home at 155 Prospect Street while claiming that the money was his.

Stucks believed there was something not right about the man with all the money in his hat, so he told Berghauser to wait inside his store for a few minutes while he went outside. Stucks then locked the door to his store and questioned the boys who had chased Berghauser. The boys said they had seen Berghauser counting a pile of bills, and that as soon as Berghauser saw them watching he gathered up the money in his hat and ran. Stucks was convinced that the money did not belong to Berhauser so he found Officer Fegenbaum of the Fifth Precinct who brought Berghauser to the station house. Berghauser immediately confessed to the desk sergeant that he had stolen the money from his employer, Urban Kneer, a cider manufacturer at 274 Houston Street in Manhattan.

Sometime during the afternoon Mr. Kneer had a large sum of money on a counter in preparation of paying a mortgage. Berghauser asked for a cup of cider, and since he was a trusted employee Kneer went down to the basement with the money out on the counter. In a moment of impulsiveness, Berghauser scooped the money into his

hat and ran. He said he had no idea where he was going
when he ran out of the store, and he ended up taking a
ferry to Brooklyn. He stopped on Wythe Avenue and sat
on a stoop counting the money until he saw the boys
watching him which prompted him to run because he
feared they were going to rob him. The three thousand
dollars Berghauser had on him was returned to Mr. Kneer,
and a repentant Berghauser was turned over to New York
detectives.[76]

THE PRECINCTS

The First Precinct included a large part of the millionaire neighborhood of the Heights, and the dry goods and other mercantile palaces of Fulton Street. With the Second Precinct it contained what was once the town of Brooklyn, and before that, the village of Breuckelen . The station house on Adams Street, near Myrtle Avenue, occupied the whole handsome new Police Court House, except the second floor. Its roll was made up of the captain, four sergeants, two roundsmen, fifty patrolmen and two doormen.

The commander of the First Precinct was Captain James Campbell, a man described as slightly above the average height, broad shouldered and finely proportioned. In 1887 he was about fifty years of age, with an honest and handsome face, and wearing a moustache, which, as well as his hair, was white. He entered the Police Department on December 10th, 1853 and was assigned to patrol duty in the Twenty Eighth Precinct, under the old Metropolitan system. His first night on post was probably the hardest ever spent during his police service. He wandered over rocks and unpaved streets, without meeting a soul from midnight until six in the morning. Two goats were all that ever disturbed the peaceful quiet of the night.

JAMES CAMPBELL,
Captain.

Campbell was promoted to roundsman and in the fall of 1869 he took a step higher, being made sergeant and assigned to the Forty-Fourth Precinct. He remained in the Fourth Precinct until the summer of 1873, when he was appointed captain, and assigned to the command of the Tenth Precinct. In 1879 he was placed in command of the First Precinct.

The Second Precinct was one of the worst precincts for crime in the city, and for years was infested by the notorious "Chain Gang," which was finally broken up by a former commanding officer, Captain Crafts. Along the river front the neighborhood was, in most part, of a hard character, especially along Freeman Street, where the sailors congregated and fought. Many factories were contained within the precinct boundaries which offered great inducements for robberies. The station house was a three-story brick building, situated on the corner of York and Jay Streets. The cells were damp, so much so, that for some time past it had not been thought humane to put prisoners in the lower tier. The station house, taken as a whole, was unworthy of the policemen who were compelled to use it as a home.

Captain John W. Eason, commanding the Second Precinct, was born in New York City, and was 43-years old in 1887. He came to Brooklyn shortly after his birth and enlisted in the Fourteenth Regiment, New York Volunteers at the start of the Civil War. He was wounded at the first battle of Bull Run, also at Antietam and Gettysburg. He was honorably discharged, June 6th, 1864. Three weeks after his discharge, he was appointed patrolman on the old Metropolitan Police force, and assigned to the Forty-First Precinct, which became the First Precinct. In May 1870, he was made acting-sergeant, and a month later appointed sergeant. On September 16th, 1881, on account of the illness of Captain Craft, he was ordered to take command of the Second Precinct.

There was no nonsense about Captain Eason. He had a plain, straight- forward way of talking directly to the point, and the meaning of what he said was never obscure. He believed in men performing their duties faithfully and with exactitude, without any attempt at evasion or skulking.

The Third Precinct encroached upon a portion of a region in which crooks of the worst character held sway, while, on the other hand, many blocks of handsome mansions and respectable dwellings were found along its streets. The station house was situated on Butler Street, just off from Court Street, and was pleasantly shaded with trees. It was well equipped and had the new patrol box system in working order. For many years, the notorious

"Smoky Hollow" was included in this precinct. It was a district equaling, if not exceeding, the "Five Points" of New York in vice and depravity. The number of crimes planned and committed by its desperate inhabitants made a large and terrible volume. Murder, assaults of the most sickening nature, heartless torture inflicted upon unfortunate victims not giving up all in their possession, even to the shoes, hat and underclothes the moment they were demanded, and all other crimes against life and property which the vilest of men and women can devise and perpetrate, formed part of this record.

The precinct grew better-behaved and more decent, and in 1887 it stood in admirable police condition. It nevertheless contained an immense population of the very poor, in which intoxication was fearfully prevalent, and in which the crimes and disorders caused by drink took place with unhappy regularity.

In 1887 the commanding officer of the Third Precinct was Captain Patrick H. Leavey. This powerfully built man with the dark complexion was born in 1843 and appointed on the police force May 7th, 1866. He was made roundsman October 12th, 1869, and sergeant June 17th, 1871. He was made captain of the precinct November 13th, 1876. Leavey deserved much of the credit for clearing out "Smoky Hollow."

Captain Leavey kept a huge scrapbook of everything that appeared in type regarding the crimes and criminals of Brooklyn and New York. Well indexed, it enabled the reader to pursue the history of any crime, or the career of a law breaker, from its start to the dismal end which always closed wrong-doing.

A case that Captain Leavey liked to talk involved a man named Billy Maloney, who became better known as "Billy the Kid." Maloney belonged to the Smoky Hollow Gang, and though neither large nor muscular he was one of its most desperate characters. He was shrewd, and kept himself out of the law's clutches for some time, but at last when a warrant was issued for him for a serious charge he left the city and traveled west and soon became one of the famous desperadoes of the old west. Leavey noted that

Maloney was killed by a fellow desperado known as Pat Garrett.

I don't necessarily want to cast doubt on Captain Leavey's tale of Billy the Kid, but there are just too many holes in his story for it to go unchallenged. Billy the Kid was born in New York City and that is one of the few facts the Captain had semi-correct. The outlaw was born on the East Side of Manhattan and there is no record of his affiliation with Brooklyn or the Smokey Hollow gang. In fact, he moved to Kansas with his parents when still a small child. Billy the Kid used the name William H. Bonney and his parents were named McCarty. I could find no record of him ever using the name Maloney. The other fact that Leavey almost got right was that Pat Garrett killed Billy the Kid, but Garrett was not a fellow desperado – he was a sheriff.

If I had to guess, I believe Billy Maloney was a Brooklyn criminal who fled the law by going out west, but that Captain Leavey got Maloney mixed up with the real Billy the Kid.

FOURTH PRECINCT. Was previously profiled.

The Fifth Precinct was located at the corner of North First Street and Bedford Avenue in a three-story brick building with brownstone trimmings. The commanding officer of the precinct in 1887, Captain Cornelius Woglom, was a master carpenter and supervised the construction of the precinct in 1859 – 1860. Woglom's experience serves as an example of the politics of the era. He had no affiliation with the police department when the precinct construction began. In fact, he was an alderman who won the contract to build the precinct. When the project was completed, Woglom decided to apply for appointment to the police department, but not just any appointment. He applied for a captain's position, and with his political influence, the man who was to become known as the "Chief of Williamsburg." received an appointment as captain with the Brooklyn Police Department.

The Fifth Precinct was described as the favorite camping ground for tramps and dissolute characters of both sexes, and seldom during the winter months did a night pass without the precinct being filled to its capacity.

The Sixth Precinct covered the section Brooklyn known as " Dutch Town," and for some reason was described as the most notable district in the country for elopements, breach-of-promise cases, divorces, lover's quarrels, and picnics.

The station house was located on the southeast corner of Stagg Street and Bushwick Avenue, with the inhabitants of the area in 1887 being described as chiefly engaged in the tailoring business, while a number of breweries gave employment to hundreds of men and boys. There were two districts, called " Picklesville " and the "Swamp," which were high crime areas.

Captain William J. Kaiser was the commanding officer of the Sixth Precinct. He was born in 1842 and when the Civil War broke out, he enlisted in the 49th New York Volunteers. He was made first lieutenant for bravery on March 1st, 1864, and on March 1st of the following year was promoted to the rank of captain for his gallant services in the battles before Petersburg. On June 7th, 1864, he was mustered out of the service. He was appointed a patrolman on the Metropolitan Police Force, June 25th, 1866, and assigned to duty in the Forty-Ninth Precinct, which became the Ninth Precinct. In June 1867, he was transferred to the Fourth Precinct, and two years later was sent to the Fifth Precinct. In May 1870, he was

made sergeant, skipping the rank of roundsman. He was
then sent to the Sixth Precinct, where he remained until
1876. He was made captain in August 1873 and
commanded the Sixth Precinct until his transfer to the
Twelfth three years later. In 1878 he was again
transferred, this time to the Thirteenth, where he remained
until being moved to the Sixth Precinct in 1880.

The Sixth Sub-Precinct was made up of a portion of
the Sixth and Seventh Precincts. It was one of the roughest
portions of Brooklyn and boasted of no wealthy streets. It
contained that portion of Brooklyn known as "The Green,"
which for years was nightly the scene of the most daring
robberies, obscene adventures and attempts at murder. The
precinct came into existence on October 12th, 1885, and in
two years over one thousand arrests were made.

The station house was on Graham Avenue, between
Frost and Richardson Streets., and the commander was
Sergeant Edmund Brown, who was described as a stout,
handsome and good-natured fellow.

The Seventh Precinct was a three-story brick
building on the corner of Greenpoint and Manhattan
Avenues. In one part of this precinct was situated what
was known as "Danger Town," inhabited by the "Far
Downs," and was at one time a very rough locality, but
when Captain Rhodes took command of the precinct, the
predators who had infested the district were driven away.

Captain George R. Rhodes was a well-preserved
man of 62-years of age in 1887. He was a fine linguist,
having traveled extensively and studied a great deal
abroad. Secretary of State Bayard was a schoolmate of his.
In 1837, at the age of twelve years, he went to Turkey,
where his father was chief naval instructor. While there he
studied and mastered the French and Italian languages, and

also learned to converse in Turkish. For three years he remained abroad until his father was transferred back to the United States.

GEORGE R. RHODES,
Captain.

On December 1, 1857, Rhodes was appointed to the Metropolitan Police Force. Four years later, on December 31,1862, he was made captain and was given command of the Third Precinct. It was there during the riots of 1863 that he proved himself a most efficient officer, rendering great service to the city in preserving order in that dangerous locality of the waterfront which was in his district.

The Eighth Precinct station house was located on the corner of Fifth Avenue and Sixteenth street, and was an imposing three-story structure of Philadelphia brick, that

made the small modest dwellings in the area look
strikingly dull and unpretentious by comparison. The
precinct was built in1873 and was considered one of the
most perfect precinct station houses in the city.

Captain Thomas Murphy was the commanding
officer of the Eighth Precinct. He was appointed
patrolman in the Fourth Precinct in 1867 and in 1870 was
made roundsman. In 1873 he was assigned to the detective
force and was promoted to sergeant in 1878 and
transferred to the Twelfth Precinct. From there he was
promoted to captain and assigned to the Eighth Precinct.

THOMAS MURPHY,
Captain.

The Eighth Sub-Precinct was an ordinary three-story
building on Third Avenue, near the corner of Thirty-fifth
Street. It had the regulation lamp on the outside and was

built of brick. The Precinct covered a large and lonesome area and was bounded by Twenty-fifth Street running northeast to Fifth Avenue, by Fifth Avenue running south to Thirty-sixth Street

The Ninth Precinct station house was located near the corner of Gates and Marcy Avenues. It was built in 1864 and was a pretentious three-story modern building of Philadelphia pressed brick, painted white, with dark red blinds and brown-stone trimmings. The precinct was a large but sparsely settled district, and it was noted that due to the intense vigilance of its police and their officers it was pretty well kept free of all kinds of obnoxious characters.

Captain James Ennis, the commanding officer of the Ninth Precinct, was born on the 1st of March 1847 and was appointed a patrolman on August 8th,1870 and assigned to the Sixth Precinct. On November 17th, 1875, he was made detective. In this capacity he served until March 1884, when he was transferred to the Thirteenth Precinct. On January 5th, 1887, he passed the civil service examination for captain with the second highest score. He was appointed Captain and assigned to the Ninth Precinct.

JAMES ENNIS,
Captain.

The Tenth Precinct was situated on the northwest corner of Bergen Street and Sixth Avenue. It was a large red brick structure, trimmed with white stone, of imposing appearance and of modern build. Both the Mounted Squad and its commanding sergeant, and the precinct officers found shelter within it and still had room to spare. It was the largest by far of any station house in the city and resembled a public building more than any of the others. To the side of the building was the stable for the horses of the Mounted Squad, in which everything was as clean and neat as in a dwelling for human beings.

Captain Henry L. Jewett was born in 1843. On April 18, 1861, at the early age of eighteen, he responded to his country's call for troops by enlisting in the Third New York Infantry and served nearly four years. In 1873 he was made drill captain at Headquarters and from 1882 to 1883 had charge of the Detective Squad. 1884 saw him appointed to the command of the Tenth Precinct. Captain Jewett was described as a prepossessing gentleman about six feet in height, rather slenderly built, wearing a light mustache. His reputation as an officer had always been excellent and he was greatly esteemed by all his men. Nothing better illustrated the Captain's kindness of character than his fondness for animals. His favorite Newfoundland dog, Minnie, lived with him at the station house and became something of a celebrity.

Minnie was an intelligent and observing dog, and always took a keen interest in the prisoners captured by the precinct officers. When any of the officers brought in a prisoner Minnie stood attentively listening to the desk sergeant taking the prisoner's pedigree, and when the sergeant ordered the arresting officer to lodge the prisoner in the cells Minnie followed at his heels and did not take her eyes off the culprit until he was safely behind bolts and bars. In one instance a prisoner appearing before the desk sergeant made a dash for liberty, whereupon Minnie, who had been quietly watching what was going on, sprang after the escaping criminal and laid such tight hold on the rear of the fellow's trousers that he was only too glad to surrender and quietly follow the officer to his cell.

The Eleventh Precinct station house was located in the center of the manufacturing district of South Brooklyn, on the corner of Van Brunt and Seabring Streets. The precinct was a four-story brick dwelling-house which formerly had been a tenement house, but on April 19, 1876, the structure was transitioned into the Eleventh Precinct. Most of the arrests in the precinct were for intoxication, assaults, burglaries committed on vessels up at the storehouses on the waterfront, and for foreign sailors carrying concealed weapons.

DANIEL J. LOWERY,
Captain.

Captain Daniel J. Lowery was horn in 1846. On October 6th, 1874, he was appointed as patrolman and assigned to the Fourth Precinct, where he remained until 1878, when he was transferred to the First Precinct. In 1881, he was promoted to roundsman and assigned to the Sixth Sub Precinct, where he remained until he was promoted to sergeant in 1885. In 1887 he was promoted to captain and placed in command of the Eleventh Precinct.

Up until 1887, Captain Lowery was one of the few captains on the force who owed their promotion from patrolman up to captain to the Civil Service Commission instead of political friends.

The Twelfth Precinct was formerly known as the Tenth Sub-Precinct. The commanding officer, Captain

William H. Folk, was born in 1837. He was the son of ex-superintendent John S. Folk, the father of the police force and one of the finest disciplinarians in its history.

WILLIAM H. FOLK,
Captain.

At the age of nineteen he was appointed clerk to the Chief of Police, on the 1st of May 1856, long before the Metropolitan Police system was established. In this position he became thoroughly acquainted with the management workings of the force. In 1858 he was made patrolman on the Metropolitan Police Force and detailed to clerical and detective duties around the Central Office. In 1862 Folk joined the 173rd Regiment of New York Volunteers and fought in the Civil War. He came back to Brooklyn when peace was restored and was reappointed to the police force and detailed to work in and around the

Central Office. In 1881, he was appointed sergeant and two days later, owing to a vacancy, was made captain.

The Thirteenth Precinct was described as being at one time a great resort for crooks and cut-throats, but by 1887 it has been transformed into an orderly, law-abiding neighborhood. It was in most part a tenement-house district, inhabited by hard working people who found employment in the many factories and breweries located in the precinct. The station house was located on Bartlet Street and Flushing Avenue.

THOMAS L. DRUHAN,
Captain.

Captain Thomas L. Druhan, the commanding officer, was described as a man of great ability and was well versed in police tactics, having attained his position through civil service examination. As a detective, Druhan had an excellent record, made many important arrests and secured a great number of convictions for every crime on record excepting murder. In 1876, he was appointed captain and assigned to command the Thirteenth Precinct, a position he still held in 1887.

The Fourteenth Precinct station house was an old-fashioned, two-story, square wooden building, with large airy rooms, and surrounded by a large garden laid out into flower beds. The Precinct, which was probably the largest in the city, was very thinly settled but covered an immense area. Many were the funeral processions which the officers of this precinct had to guard as they wound their way to "The Evergreens," the beautiful City of the Dead. Its grassy plots and stately monuments, its perfumed flower beds and sanded walks were daily the scene of the last sad rites that love can offer to death.

The smiling countenance and imposing figure of
Captain James Dunn were well-known to every man,
woman and child in the Fourteenth Precinct. Born on May
3, 1838, this popular officer came to Brooklyn when very
young and attended the city public school. His friends
urged him to go on the police force in 1866, and on August
23rd he received an appointment as a patrolman. On June
11, 1870, his popularity forced him over several
roundsmen, and he was made sergeant.

Captain Dunn preserved strict discipline in his
command, but he was known to look the other way when
an indiscretion was committed by one special member of

his precinct. In fact, this member of the precinct was exempt from wearing a uniform and was not required to perform regular patrol duty. This member seemed to exert so much influence over Captain Dunn that he was permitted to do exactly what he pleased, without suffering any penalties. The name of this privileged character was "Billy," and he was found by Captain Dunn on a wintery night several years ago on the outskirts of the city, half hidden in the snow. "Billy" did not carry a stick and he walked on four legs. "Billy" was a goat. His only duty consisted of guarding the orchard surrounding the station house from the ravages of mischievous small boys.

The Fifteenth Precinct was located on Congress Street near Columbia Street, in the heart of what was known as " Smoky Hollow," in a three-story brick building which was used up to 1881 as a tenement house. When this building was first turned into a police-station it was an off-shoot of the First Precinct and was termed the Third Sub-Precinct. On July14, 1885, it was made a full precinct.

Captain Henry Kellett was born in 1838. At the outbreak of the Civil War, he enlisted in the Thirteenth Regiment of Brooklyn. Shortly after his discharge he was appointed to the police force, but he experienced trouble from a war wound and resigned after serving for only two months. In 1867 he was again appointed patrolman and assigned to the Forty-third Precinct. He remained in that assignment until the Metropolitan Police disbanded. He was then assigned to Brooklyn. In 1872 he was promoted sergeant. On June 14, 1885, he was appointed captain of the Fifteenth Precinct.

HENRY KELLETT,
Captain.

The Sixteenth Precinct station house was marked by a bright colored lamp in the front of one of a row of tenement houses on Clymer Street, near Kent Avenue.

Captain John Brennan was born on November 10th, 1834, and on November18, 1862 he was appointed as patrolman. After four years as patrolman, he was promoted roundsman. While obeying the commands of the "Chief of Williamsburg" (Captain Woglom) in 1867 he was appointed Sergeant. On July 15, 1885 he took captain's rank. Captain Brennan averaged from eight hundred to nine hundred arrests a year, which made his name a terror to the criminal classes of his neighborhood.

JOHN BRENNAN,
Captain.

The Seventeenth Precinct: When the Metropolitan Police District was abolished in 1870 New Lots was left without police protection. The Brooklyn Police Bill was amended so as to give authority to the Town Board to apply to the Police Commissioner of the City of Brooklyn, under a requisition, for the appointment of as many policemen as it was deemed necessary. Under this authority the Town Board of New Lots in 1871 made application for the appointment of three officers. There was no station house for these men to report to, but this was the beginning of what would eventually become the Seventeenth Precinct.

Captain Henry French was born in 1849 and appointed to the police force in 1876. When the city refused to give police protection to New Lots, French, who was then a patrolman, resigned and upon the organization of the New Lots Police Department accepted a re-appointment, this time his position being that of a sergeant. He became captain when the town became annexed to Brooklyn.

HENRY FRENCH,
Captain.

In 1877 the precinct was almost entirely rural. Many of its people engaged in tailoring and light manufacturing, but a very large number were farmers and gardeners. Its policing situation was excellent, with the chief source of trouble being visitors from the other sections of Brooklyn and from New York.[77]

RAYMOND STREET JAIL

We have talked about how the men of the Brooklyn Police Department worked to keep the streets of the city free from predators, but where did these criminals go after being apprehended by the police.

In the 1880s Fort Greene was described as one of the loveliest spots in Brooklyn. It had graceful rolling hills with velvet lawns, vigorous trees and shrubbery, and serpentine walks. It was there that Washington made his last stand against the British conquest of Long Island. At the northwest corner stood an irregular pile of granite buildings and enclosing walls. This was the Raymond Street Jail.

Prior to 1836 the site was occupied by a crude "lockup" or "coop" that provided very limited prisoner security. As Brooklyn grew so did the criminal population along with the need for a larger, more secure jail.

In 1887 the new jail was built of granite. It was three stories high with a separate women's jail and was completely surrounded by a wall. Entering the jail at the main entrance led to a short hall that crossed another at right angles. On the left was the warden's private office, while just beyond was the door leading to the jail yard and the women's prison.

On the second floor were the sheriff's quarters while the third-floor housed prisoners for debt and included the living apartment of the warden.

The actual jail utilized a two-block system of four tiers or galleries, containing 432-cells. Each 8-foot by 5-foot cell was ventilated and provided with a cot and sanitary facilities. The lower floor was used for prisoners in bad health but not sick enough to be sent to the hospital.

The women's prison was actually an old building that had been formerly used as a courthouse and meeting place for the Board of Supervisors. In 1887 the inside of the women's prison was all new and divided into square halls lettered from A to F. These halls contained eighteen rooms, each opening one into the other. Every room contained six iron beds, with mattress, sheets and blankets.

The first floor was for unruly prisoners, while the second floor was for prisoners awaiting trial, and the third floor for short-time prisoners. Heavily barred iron doors connected the halls with the stairway, but other than that, inmates were without restriction.

In 1887 the capacity of the jail was 682 prisoners – 432 males and 250 females. The prisoners were mostly from the City of Brooklyn although there were usually some inmates brought from New York and other cities to await trial. The jail was used for both criminal and civil cases, as during this era a person could be arrested for civil offenses such as slander or libel.

The inmate day began at 6:30 AM. Breakfast consisted of a quart of coffee and a half pound of bread. All prisoners were then turned out of their cells and marched to the tubs where each prisoner was compelled to wash thoroughly, with soap and towels being furnished in abundance. A short time was then provided for exercise before the prisoners were returned to their cells. A certain number of prisoners were assigned housework in lieu of returning to the cell.

Visiting days were Thursdays and Sundays between two and four o'clock in the afternoon. On the other days of the week some visitors were admitted by passes issued by the undersheriff.

On regular visiting days the crowds were in the hundreds and comprised people from all walks of life. At two o'clock sharp a keeper swung open the large oak door at the main entrance. At five o'clock the visitors were ordered to leave and an hour later the inmates received dinner, which was the same meal they enjoyed for breakfast.

Old offenders sometimes treated their incarceration as a joke and passed their time with profane conversation. Others begged for reading materials and tried to bury their thoughts in books. Another class of inmate tried to while away the time with sleep or in some activity that required careful attention. One particular German who would regularly receive ten-day sentences for disorder and drunkenness consumed every spare minute of his time in jail building full rigged ships inside narrow mouthed bottles. The short-term prisoners constituted a large majority of the inmate population. Most were sentenced for drunkenness, assault, or disorderly conduct.

In 1887 it was the feeling that there was little hope of rehabilitating these short-term prisoners. The incorrigible nature of these offenders was confirmed at the time through studies by experts like Dr. M. Dugdale, who once said before the Brooklyn Philosophical Society: "After many years the action of the alcohol and the habits produced by its use are no longer resisted by the human system but affect the confirmed drunkard organically. He undergoes a change and can no longer modify his second nature, but remains a charge upon society all his life, and, transmitting his tendencies to the next generation, creates a new set of drunkards for which the State is compelled to make provisions."[78]

With experts like Dr. Dugdale, there didn't seem to be too much emphasis placed on rehabilitation during the latter part of the 19th century.

POLICE DISCIPLINE

Researching this book confirmed a universal truth for me. No matter the century, police officers work tirelessly and heroically to keep the citizenry safe. The police are also a microcosm of the society they work in. In large cities, such as Brooklyn in the late part of the 19th century, there was a small portion of the population that were criminals. Accordingly, there was also a very small segment of the police population partaking in misconduct and criminal acts. What I found very interesting was how much of the crime and misconduct, whether committed by an average citizen or a police officer, had the element of alcohol involved with the act.

The Commissioner of Police was given a quasi-judicial authority in order to preserve the discipline of the force. This authority comprised bringing a member of the police before him, examining under oath and punishing by reprimand, degradation, fine, suspension and dismissal.

Complaints against officers were made primarily by fellow members of the force, usually superior officers, and rarely by private citizens. The majority were for slight infractions of the rules of the department, a goodly number for entering saloons or drinking, while on duty, many for conduct unbecoming an officer and very few for serious offences.

Violations of the rules were a common occurrence; in fact, they were unknowingly committed by the best men of the force. Thus, in the case of the Wise robbery, a burglary that was perpetrated after midnight by expert thieves of the best class, the fact was not discovered by the police until the following morning. This being technically an infraction of the rules, the captain preferred charges against the sergeant and two officers, who were tried, found guilty and dismissed! After a few days had passed, however, they were reinstated and treated with the same respect as if nothing had happened. It seemed unjust, at first sight, to make the non-discovery of a crime an offence on the part of an officer on duty, but it had been found by long experience to be the only method of securing and preserving a high discipline and esprit de corps.

That last statement regarding "spirit de corps" left me shaking my head. I can't imagine working under rules and regulations that would result in termination if a crime occurred on my post and the perpetrator was not arrested.

Along with this rule should be placed those which require explanation from a patrolman for absence from his post, for not wearing gloves on certain occasions, for carelessness in dress, for being a minute late, and all similar regulations. Violations of these minor rules were punished by reprimand and forfeiture of pay, seldom exceeding five days' salary. In those cases, it was often difficult to tell truth from false hood. For example, a policeman was called by a friendly proprietor to eject a "fighting drunk" from a saloon. He enters the place and awes the would- be pugilist into abject contrition. The other guests intercede, and he departs. Or maybe the real story was that the policeman entered the saloon, took a drink, and departed. In both cases he was seen by his roundsman, who lodged a complaint against him. The testimony against him was the same in both cases. Generally, the second case is what occurred, and generally the first case is alleged in his defense. The commissioner in such cases depended largely upon the appearance, habits, and record of the accused. If these were good, the complaint was dismissed - if bad, he was reprimanded or fined.

The rules were at times taken advantage of by people to gratify their malice against officers they disliked. One officer was brought before the board five times in three months by a liquor dealer whose license he had caused to be revoked. Against a patrolman whom he hated, an unscrupulous roundsman brought ten charges of this class. In the last case he tried to strengthen his complaint by false swearing but was detected and expelled from the force.

Drinking was another fruitful cause of trouble for policemen. The prevalent vice of the American people, drink and drunkenness, was, it must be confessed, passed into the ranks of the police and there worked the same damage it did everywhere. While an officer who drank in moderation could do his duty properly, (this was the feeling in 1887 – not today) the slightest excess rendered him unfit to be a policeman. For this reason, the rules were stringent against drinking and intoxication. They were obeyed by nearly all the members of the police. But there were black sheep in every flock, and the policeman who yielded to temptation was regularly brought before the board

Under the category of conduct unbecoming an officer the Commissioner had a wide range of latitude. Discourtesy to private citizens, insults or insulting language, challenges to fight, threats to inflict physical or other injury, neglect of wife or children, profanity and disorderly conduct, were a few of the long list of unseemly acts which were covered. This rule had also been construed to include the deliberate non-payment of just debts by extravagant officers. It was therefore popular with tradesmen and impecunious doctors and dentists. The procedure was somewhat peculiar. If the officer admitted the debt, he was ordered to pay it off by monthly installments. If he denied the debt or disputed the account between himself and the creditor, the Commissioner dismissed the case and relegated the case to the civil courts. [79]

So, what were some of the shenanigans Brooklyn police officers were disciplined for during the late 19th century?

On May 30th, 1878, Officer Francis May, of the Twelfth Precinct, was dismissed from the force for buying in a liquor store in uniform, and for assisting a citizen to help two women over a fence. I can understand the problem with buying liquor, but I would need more information to understand the problem with helping two women over a fence.

On June 19th, 1878, the Police Commissioners dismissed from the force Officer Thomas Hart, of the 9th Sub-Precinct, for playing cards in a saloon on Gates Avenue and Broadway. While under the influence of liquor Hart assaulted James Smith during an argument during a game of sucre.[80]

During July of 1879 Patrolman Michael Travers, of the Second Precinct, made an exhibition of himself in a Fulton Street liquor saloon. According to the report of Captain Crafts, of the Second Precinct, Travers landed on Jewell's Wharf at 7:40 PM after disembarking from a Rockaway steamboat. He seemed under the influence of stimulants and crossed the gang plank singing. Travers went directly into Martin Maddigan's liquor saloon, at 9 Fulton Street, where he ordered drinks, and continued imbibing until he owed eighty cents. A demand was then made for the money, but Travers declined to pay any attention to it. The bartender, however, insisted on payment which so angered Travers that he drew a pistol and threatened to shoot the bartender. The loud and excited tones in which the conversation was carried on had fortunately attracted the attention of Sergeant Carrougher, of the Second Precinct, who was passing, and he entered the saloon just at the critical moment, and seeing the situation, attempted to arrest Travers. The intoxicated officer was furious and declined to submit to arrest, offering a furious resistance to the sergeant. Sensing the danger, Carrougher rapped for help, and in a few minutes four officers responded. A desperate tussle, almost amounting to a fight took place, and in the melee the sergeant was four times by mistake struck in the face by an outsider, who pretended that he was assisting the police. Officer Kearney also had his coat badly torn, but finally, superior force prevailed, and Travers was taken to the station house and locked up on a charge of drunkenness and disorderly conduct. The next morning the prisoner was taken before Justice Walsh and upon complaint of Sergeant Carrougher and was sentenced to pay a fine of $10 or spend ten days in jail. A friend paid the fine and Travers was liberated, but not off the hook. Superintendent Campbell suspended Travers from duty and ordered departmental charges to be preferred against him.

Travers' record as a member of the police force was not good. He was born in January 1851 and learned the trade of an oysterman. On December 6, 1876, he obtained an appointment as patrolman, and was assigned to duty in the Third Precinct in 1879. During 1877 his conduct, according to the records, appeared to have been exemplary, as no charges were preferred against him by his commanding officer, but since then he had eleven charges preferred against him. In 1878 he was fined as follows by the Commissioners for offences:

- For violation of rules, one day's pay, January 9
-Two days' pay April 4; for improper conduct
-One day's pay, October 1; for violation of rules
-Two days' pay, October 1; for neglect of duty
-One day's pay, November 6 for neglect of duty
-Three days' pay December 11 for neglect of duty
-On the 9th of April he was fined one day's pay for neglect of duty.

Due to his record and his drunken brawl arrest, Travers was dismissed from the police force, but his troubles didn't end there. On July 25th, 1882, ex-policeman Michael Travers was seen by Officer McDermott of the Third Precinct, on Columbia Street, drunk and acting in a disorderly manner. McDermott requested him to move on, and he told the officer to go to hell, and that he had money enough to pay any fine a judge might place upon him. Travers was arrested and admitted to Justice Bergan that he made the remark attributed to him. Travers was truthful in one sense. He did have the ten dollars necessary to pay the fine imposed.

On January 5th, 1882, Officer Bernard Riley, of the Third precinct, was found helplessly drunk by Roundsman Downey. Riley was taken to the station house in a wagon because he was unable to walk. Riley also attempted to assault the roundsman at the station house. Riley denied the attempted assault and said he had been invited by a friend to have a New Year drink, and that he only took two glasses of whiskey. Commissioner Jourdan dismissed Riley from the force.

On March 16th, 1882, Patrolman George W. Travis, of the Seventh Precinct, was found on his post at Franklin

Street and Greenpoint Avenue too drunk to walk and was taken in charge by two other officers, who took him to the station house where he was stripped of his uniform and placed in a cell.

Commanding a police precinct can be an extremely stressful occupation, one whose success is largely based on the motivation and skill of the police officers working in the precinct. Precinct commanders must keep close watch for the incompetent, lazy, unmotivated officers who can affect the performance and morale of the entire command. These officers with negative attitudes are a threat to the success of the precinct commander. This is a career threat, not a physical threat; that is, unless one of the officers in the precinct was named Maurice Heffernan.

In 1878 the description of an effective police officer was a bit odd. 37-year-old Maurice Heffernan, of the First Precinct had been a patrolman with the Brooklyn Police Department since 1870. He was described as an excellent officer with the exception that he would go on a spree from time to time and neglect his duty for two or three days. Prior to the incident about to be described Heffernan had twenty charges preferred against him. Evidently, the bar wasn't set too high at that time to be considered an excellent officer.

On April 30th the men of the precinct, including Heffernan received their monthly pay. Heffernan was not seen again until the morning of May 3rd. In the interim, Captain Joel Smith, the commanding officer of the First Precinct and the oldest captain on the force, dispatched a police surgeon to Heffernan's home thinking that the officer may be sick. All the other times Heffernan had gone missing was due to intoxication, and when he reported for duty of the morning of May 3rd, he admitted he had been in a state of intoxication for the prior two days. The next day Heffernan was served with charges for neglect of duty.

On May 5th, just after 1 PM Heffernan entered the precinct with the rest of the platoon to prepare to go off duty. Captain Smith was standing near the front desk and Sgt. Walsh was the desk officer. Heffernan did not say a word as he went directly upstairs with the rest of the officers. When the bell sounded notifying the incoming platoon that they were dismissed to go home, Heffernan came downstairs. Captain Smith was standing at the end of the sergeant's desk, reading a letter with one arm resting on the telegraph box. Sergeant Walsh rang the bell directing the officers to fall in for muster. As Heffernan approached the area where the Captain was standing he held a pistol in his right hand, a fact that caused no immediate concern because men were always hurrying to avoid being late and were frequently compelled to adjust their equipment while moving towards the muster. Instead of falling into line, however, Heffernan stopped by the railing in front of Captain Smith and said, "This is a nice job you have put up on me, you old bastard."

The Captain turned and saw the pistol pointed at his head. He ducked just as the weapon discharged, and the bullet struck him in the neck. As he scrambled to take cover behind the desk, Smith tripped on the rug and fell. A second bullet whistled over him and struck the door of a closet on the other side of the room. At that instant, Patrolmen Reilly, Quinn, and White jumped on Heffernan and disarmed him.

Captain Smith was carried to his office and laid on a lounge. Smith obviously believed his wound was serious, for he exclaimed, "I'm done for. God help my wife and little child."

Several police surgeons were on the scene quickly. They found the wound to be serious, but not life-threatening. The Captain was removed to his residence at 37 Tillary Street and Heffernan was arrested. When he appeared before Judge Moore, Heffernan appeared very nervous, as if he had finally recovered from the effects of alcohol. When the complaint was read to him, Heffernan said nothing, so the judge said he was entering a not guilty plea on his behalf.[81]

Finally, Heffernan made a statement on his own behalf. He said that Captain Smith had something against him and did not treat him like the rest of the men. He claimed that there was no better officer than him – when he was sober. Heffernan said he was not like the men who drank three or four time a week, and that he only drank once in three months. He admitted that when he did drink, he had a problem. "It was this bloody bock beer that spoilt me," he exclaimed. "I'm sorry for my poor family," he continued. "My old mother is outside, and I'm afraid that it will kill her. The Captain has made a good many charges against me for intoxication. The other day I reported sick to Dr. Hopkins who called on me twice but found me out. The second time I went to see him, and he ordered me on duty at 6 AM on Friday. I obeyed and after 12 o'clock on Saturday I got copies of charges made against me by the Captain. I should have gotten them a day earlier so as to give a man a chance to see his friends. There were three specifications – one for reporting sick and being drunk. I had not been drunk and I expected this would break me, which would leave me without a home for my wife and five little children. I did the shooting under the impulse of the moment. We are not allowed to carry pistols on duty in the daytime, and I borrowed this pistol from another man's closet. I meant to bring it back when I returned from home, but I had no time to put it in my pocket when the sergeant's bell rang. I had no intention of using the weapon when I spoke to him, but the sight of him excited me. I did it before I thought. You never heard a man balloo as he did about his wife and child, but he never thought anything about mine likely to be turned out into the street."

How could an "excellent" officer like Heffernan had been allowed to remain on the job and finally be in a position to shoot his commanding officer. The answer lies at least partially in the politics of the era. Heffernan was a Democrat and there were stories that he obtained his appointment through the highest influences in Tammany Hall. Captain Smith, on the other hand, was a Republican, and Heffernan may have felt secure in his assault on the Captain because it was no secret that Tammany Democrats were more than annoyed that Smith had been retained when they were seeking a captain's position for a Democrat.

After a short trial and a brief deliberation, the jury found Heffernan guilty. Judge Moore sentenced Heffernan to seven years in prison.[82]

There are concepts that remain consistent throughout the centuries. One such concept is that fact that the coverup is always worse than the crime. All too often police officers become involved in incidents where they are at fault, but only serve to compound their culpability by trying to cover up their actions. Such was the case for Brooklyn Patrolman Edward Hennessey in 1878

Officer Hennessey reported that while patrolling on Greenpoint Avenue at about 10:30 PM, a man who was about 150-yards behind him drew a pistol and shot at him, wounding him in his lower left hip. Hennessey was able to make it to the station house where Dr. Jenkens was summoned to remove the bullet. The doctor reported the injury to be a flesh wound and stated that the bullet had entered the officer's hip on a downward angle. Hennessey further stated that he had chased the shooter along Greenpoint Avenue and lost him when he ran over the Blissville Bridge. Captain Rhodes, Hennessey's commanding officer, became suspicious because the more the officer related the details of the incident, the more the story changed. Captain Rhodes continued to investigate the incident and found a man who was with Hennessey at the time he was shot. This man said that Hennessey was wounded when he accidentally shot himself with his own pistol. Hennessey was charged for making the false statement regarding the shooting and was dismissed from the force.

Apparently, Edward Hennessey's life began to spiral downward, as the ex-police officer was arrested in a beastly state of intoxication for being disorderly and breaking the doors and windows in the residence of his wife's mother about six months after his dismissal from the police department.[83]

THE TELEGRAPH BUREAU

One of the most important and useful adjuncts to the police force was the Telegraph Bureau, which during its infancy was considered one of the best managed and equipped in the world. When it was first established in 1854, with its headquarters in the basement of the City Hall, it boasted of just one Robinson dial instrument, with its slow method of transmitting orders and messages from one station to another by electric bells. One continuous circuit connected the ten precincts that existed in Brooklyn at the time. Detectives detailed from the several precincts and headquarters had charge of the operation under George H. Flanley's supervision.

In 1887 the Bureau was located in the Municipal Building, with Frank C. Mason as its superintendent. George H. Flanley resigned three years earlier after thirty years of faithful duty. Mason was a thorough electrician, and kept the system in such a condition, that a break lasting more than five minutes was almost an impossibility. Two bright, well-furnished rooms constituted the suites of offices, while all about the walls the electric paraphernalia showed the extent of the work done by the force of men constituting the corps of operators.

For a number of years after the Bureau was established, the facilities for the transmission of messages were extremely small. Now and then when a new precinct or sub-precinct was added to the original ten, another dial would be placed in position at headquarters. When the building on the corner of Livingston and Court Streets was occupied by the department, the force of operators was increased.

In the early days of the Bureau, when an order was to be sent to a precinct, the operator would call it up by so many taps on the dial, which would be responded to; and then followed the long method of so many bells, meaning some word or sentence. If it was a general order, by means of manipulating the plugs in the switch-board, all the stations were communicated with at once . If one precinct desired another, it was obtained by joining two circuits together. This placed eight or ten precincts on the same line and kept up a continual clanging of a gong in all the station houses, enough to disturb the sergeant on duty and the prisoners calmly sleeping in the cells below. Even in 1877 the old dial system was occasionally used in the transmission of some general order or a fire alarm.

In the fall of 1883, the telephone found its way into police work. It consisted of a line between Police Headquarters in New York City and Brooklyn. It was found to work so well that a new wire was run separate from headquarters to each precinct in the city. In October a new switchboard was placed in position, and another line, making three in all, built to every station. It worked admirably, and shortened the time consumed in giving orders from nine to two minutes, which, in cases requiring dispatch, often resulted in the capture of some important criminal or shortened the worriment of some mother, wife or sister, whose child, husband or brother, had fallen sick, or into the hands of miscreants.

Key to the effective operation of the system was the lineman, whose only duty was to attend to breaks in the wires. The building of new lines and the maintenance of the batteries was performed by third parties. Most of the linemen with the bureau spent over twenty years on the job, and had a complete knowledge of police subjects in general. Until the second of May 1887, the telegraph deputies were not legally connected with the police force, but on that day a bill was signed by Governor Hill, which not only brought them within the protection of the civil service law, but entitled them to be retired on a pension, as were the regular members of the force. An examination for a position as operator in the civil service routine, was one of the most difficult on the list. No one but an experienced police official could answer the first questions regarding the routine police duties, and only a good telegraph operator had a knowledge of the telephone, telegraph and switchboard workings.

The corps of operators was divided into three sections, each working eight hours. The squad on duty from eight in the morning until four in the afternoon was called the "Day Accommodation." The next section was on duty from four in the afternoon until midnight and was known as the "Evening Express." The "Owl Train" whistled "off brakes" at midnight and connected with the "Day Accommodation" at eight in the morning. The men on these trains were never employed on the same work two weeks in succession but changed from the switchboard to the record book, and thence to the daily blotter, in which was kept a full detailed account of everything that happened in the existing twenty-four hours. [84]

THE PATROL WAGON

In November 1886, the Police Commissioners put the first police patrol wagon into commission, and stabled it in Union Alley, near Myrtle Avenue. The system, though new to Brooklyn, had been tried with great success in both Philadelphia and Chicago. The wagon had not been in commission two hours before it received a telephone call from the First Precinct, to hurry to the corner of Gold Street and Myrtle Avenue. The distance of over five blocks was covered in less than three minutes. On the corner lay a man beastly intoxicated. The system used to get the unconscious man into the wagon was applied on this occasion. First, the officer in the wagon hooked his fingers into the prisoner's collar and lifted him into the wagon, where he was laid at full length on the floor. This maneuver did not take more than a minute, and before the tailboard was again placed into position, the wagon started for the station house, while the clang, clang of the big gong, manipulated by the driver's foot, warned the pedestrians and vehicles ahead to move out of the way.

In 1887 the patrol wagon squad consisted of William Dunham, J. F. Burnes, George Campbell, and Michael J. Ambro. All four were appointed from the regular force. They liked the work better than post duty and told some very interesting and humorous stories relating to the arrests made since the wagon's advent, especially during the first two or three weeks of active service.

One night in December of 1886, "Paddy" Dowd, a Fifth Ward politician, got into a dispute, and having had too much to drink, fell into the sheltering arms of a First Precinct policeman. The patrol wagon was sent to bring in the intoxicated "Paddy," who, thinking it a new service provided by the police to friendly politicians, climbed in and asked to be taken to the Bridge. When he arrived at the station house, he refused to get out, saying he wanted to go to the Bridge, even offering to pay his fare. "I'm a sucker," he said, as he fumbled for a stray nickel. Of course, force was used, and as he screamed for help, the officers dropped him over the tailboard.

About six o'clock another morning, Dunham and Burnes were sitting in the stable trying to keep awake, when the telephone rang. It was a call to the most distant box in the precinct, Hudson Avenue and Nassau Street. The morning was bitter cold, and the snow creaked beneath the wheels of the wagon, as it hurried along. On the corner in question was found a woman, lying full length in the snow, drunk and almost nude. She refused to dress. Nothing could persuade her, and she howled and yelled at the top of her voice, arousing the entire neighborhood. Dunham hurried the horse, and in about nine minutes they arrived at the station house. The woman was carried inside, and Burnes said he could have taken the whole affair as a good joke and thought nothing more about it if she had not perspired to such an extent that big beads of the fluid stood out upon her forehead and all over her body.

About the heaviest load the wagon carried was one morning when seven officers captured eight burglars in a Fifth Ward cellar. The entire party was brought to the station house without any uncomfortable crowding. "But the best joke of all," said driver Dunham, "is when we captured four or five drunks on one trip. It just made me think of a can of worms when you go fishing, to see them all on the floor of the wagon, squirming about to get in a comfortable position."[85]

POLICE PATROL.

PATROL BOXES

For years the police authorities of Brooklyn had fully recognized the importance of providing some means of instant communication between the station houses and officers on post. In the early part of the summer of 1886, the work of constructing patrol boxes in the First Precinct was commenced and when the first day of August arrived, sixteen were put in working order.

The system in use was the Gamewell, the same as was employed in Chicago. It consisted of a circular iron box about three feet in diameter, and seven feet high, painted green. Inside this box could be found a telephone and a dial box, similar to the ones that were used by the American District Telegraph Company only on a much larger scale and with a bell on top. This was used to inform the officer on post that his signal has been heard by the roundsman in the station house. The dials in the iron boxes were faced with block rubber on which was printed the several calls. A lever projected from the right of the dial, which when pressed down and then released printed on a tape at the station house, the number of the box from which the call was sent. That informed the roundsman that the officer had made an arrest and wanted the patrol wagon. The roundsman then pressed a button on his desk which rang the bell previously mentioned. That done, the arresting officer telephoned to the stable, notifying the need for the wagon.

In case the officer wished to use the telephone, an indicator on the dial was pushed one point to the left and the lever pressed as before. The ticker then registered the number of the box, with one dash following. For example, let's use box No. 27 at the corner of Washington and Nassau Streets. If the policeman wished to quell a riot or disturbance of any magnitude, he moved the indicator another point to the left and the call is printed 27. The next point was for an ambulance. It registered 27 Fire, 27 and a test call 27. If any further information was desired or wished to be transmitted to the station, the telephone was used.

The patrol boxes could only be used by the officers of the precinct who carried the keys. If a citizen discovered a fire or any other disturbance requiring police assistance, he had to find an officer, who communicated with the station house.

Each patrolman was required to report hourly from the box on his post. If there were two, he had to send in his "O. K." first from one and then the other. This broke up the old way of an officer taking a quiet doze in some convenient stable or saloon and kept him constantly, though at times unwillingly on the alert for law breakers. Patrolmen were given ten minutes grace in making his report. If it was exceeded, an account had to be rendered to the sergeant at the desk when the officers' rounds were ended.

The consummation of this great improvement was hailed with satisfaction by everybody connected with the Police Department. It greatly improved the efficiency of the force and rendered the way of the criminal harder than it had been. [86]

CRIMINAL TOOLS OF THE TRADE

In the office of the District Attorney was kept a collection of miscellaneous articles taken from criminals since 1850. These articles were called "the deodands." This word was what police called the instruments used in murders and other crimes, whether they were axes, hammers, daggers, or anything used to snuff out human life, burglar's tools, or anything else used in the commission of a crime.

Deodand was a very old term imported from England in the days before there was a Great Britain. During the dominance of the church in England all weapons used in murders fell into the possession of the church, including any horses, cattle, and other animals that had destroyed life. They were given to God or "Deo-dandus," and sold for the benefit of the church. When Henry VIII ascended to the throne and the church lost its dominance, these things were turned over to the state and deodand was the word used to describe them.[87]

Because the custom was profitable, it continued in the pre-revolution American colonies. After the United States gained independence the people took the place of the king, and the police and District Attorney became the custodians of the articles forfeited. In Brooklyn in 1887 it was confined to weapons, burglar's tools, illegal goods, and many objects related or belonging to crimes and criminals.

The deodands comprised over fifteen hundred burglar tools and instruments of destruction. The articles were contained in a handsome cabinet and were interesting though ghastly. They were numbered to correspond with the pages of a catalogue, in which the facts of the crimes were related. Directly in the center of the cabinet were hung fine pieces of white cardboard, on which were strung thirty strange-looking glass tubes. These tubes were discolored, as though burned, but the black spots were small particles of arsenic found by means of these tubes in the stomachs of the two wives of Groblewski, who was committed to the lunatic asylum for his insane act.

Joseph Groblewski was a Polish immigrant and a saloon keeper who was convicted of murdering his second wife through the use of arsenic. He was sentenced to death, but that conviction was overturned on appeal, and he was determined to be insane. Ultimately, Groblewski died in the asylum, but it is interesting to note that his first wife also died due to arsenic in her system. What a coincidence!

To the right of the cardboards were two photographs of Gonzales and Pellicer, who on the night of November 23, 1865, killed their companion, Don Jose Garcia Otero, in City Park, near the Navy Yard, and robbed him of nearly twenty-five thousand dollars. The murderers were afterwards captured, and on October 12, 1866, hung in Raymond Street Jail. I mentioned this crime earlier in the book.

In another part of the collection were a group of knives, used by Andreas Fuchs, in the performance of one of the dastardliest crimes ever committed. On January28, 1876, some children playing among the piles of lumber in the yard of Englis & Son, shipbuilders, found between one of the piles and the fence, a bloody human head, wrapped in the fragments of a German newspaper. The police were notified, and an investigation was immediately begun. The head was identified as belonging to William Simmons, an axle maker, who had worked in the foundry of Jones & Henry, in Greenpoint. Inquiry revealed the fact that

Simmons had a friend named Andreas Fuchs, whom he had been in the habit of visiting at 92 North Third Street.

Fuchs was arrested, and the detectives went to his apartment in the hope of discovering some evidence of his guilt. The result of the search was most revolting. In various portions of the room occupied by Fuchs were found pieces of human flesh and dismembered portions of a human body. A trunk was also found filled with the ghastly particles. The murderer confessed that he had killed Simmons, but it was after he had discovered that the latter was having improper relations with his wife. On the eleventh of April, Fuchs was found guilty of murder, and sentenced to be hanged. His sentence was afterwards commuted to imprisonment for life. After a short stay in prison, he became violently insane, and was removed to the State Asylum.

A blood- stained bed slat rested in one corner of the cabinet. With this instrument, James Flaherty killed his drunken wife in the rear of 96 North Fifth Street, on the September 18, 1882. He was arrested, found guilty of murder in the second degree, and sent to Sing Sing for life.

Number one hundred and sixty-one was an innocent-looking hammer, but upon investigation it turned out to be the instrument used by John M. Wright in the killing of Bernard Feron, a junkman. For this crime Wright got a life sentence. Immediately below hung, suspended by a cord, an object, one would suppose to be the bone of some animal, but which in the book of facts was said to be a part of Feron's skull. Another interesting relic was the cart-rung used by Henry Rodgers, a member of the "Battle Row Gang," in the murder of Officer John Donohue, on the seventh of July 1872. The blow must have been a terrific one, as the weapon was split in four places. Attached to the rung was a telegram from Governor Hoffman denying a stay of execution for Rodgers, who was hung on December 6, 1872.

So, what became of these artifacts that were an important part of Brooklyn's history of policing? Nobody seems to know. In 1924 a reporter approached District Attorney Charles J. Dodd and asked to view the deodands. Dodd said he had a vague memory of there being a metal case containing the artifacts when he took office. He said he became tired of looking at them and he believed former District Attorney Clarke had told the courthouse janitor to take them away and that he did not care what became of them. They were bound together as rubbish and for a long time lay in the cellar of the county courthouse, likely falling into the hands of the trash removal man. The bottom line was that there was no trace of any of the gruesome reminders of early crime in Brooklyn.[88]

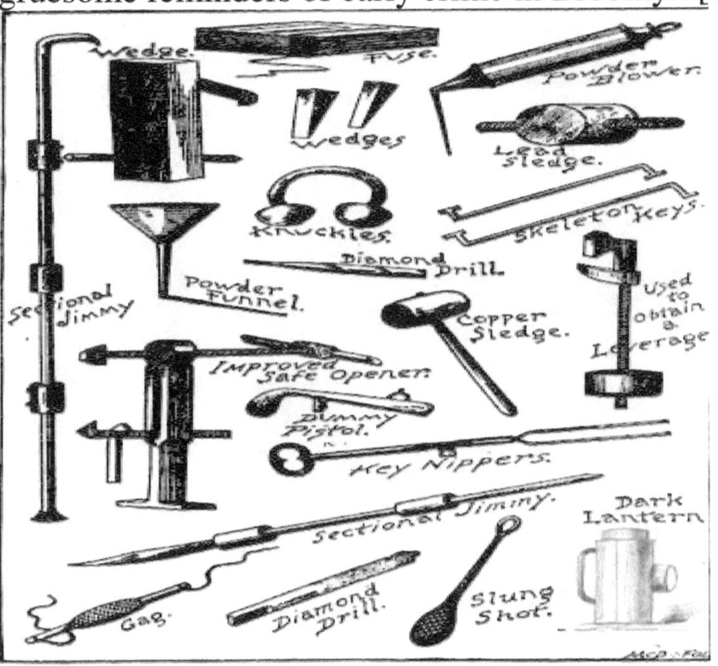

THE MOUNTED SQUAD

In 1875, General Jourdan, the Police Commissioner, established the Mounted Squad with ten men. The squad was placed under the command of Sergeant John H. Johnson, whose military experience and knowledge of veterinary surgery made him a perfect choice for the role.

The Squad made its headquarters at the Tenth Precinct station house on the corner of Sixth Avenue and Bergen Street, just off Flatbush Avenue, Brooklyn's favorite road to Coney Island and Sheepshead Bay. The stables were situated next door on Sixth Avenue. They were fronted by a well-paved and exquisitely clean yard and consisted of a handsome two-story brick building trimmed with brown stone. The floor was flush with the level of the street, so that the horses could go and come without any step or incline to stumble over. The ground floor was one large room and contained a small office in front and stalls on either side.

The squad was composed of ten patrolmen and as many horses. They made two rounds a day and none at night because the traffic on the roads at night was so small as to be insignificant. Their chief duties were to prevent rapid driving and racing in the streets, and when necessary to arrest the offenders, to stop runaways and to assist the injured and protect property when collisions or accidents occurred.

The mounted officer developed a special bond with his horse. He washed and groomed the horse, nursed them when sick, and played with them in leisure moments. The horses seemed to appreciate the dangers and duties of their position and were extremely careful as to both themselves and their rider in approaching and pursuing a thief. Sergeant Johnson said of the horses: "If my horses could only talk, they'd make much better policemen than many men who come here and bore us with their ignorance." [89]

The main function of the Mounted Squad was to respond to runaway horses. If a horse ran away, a policeman on foot could do nothing to stop it in the vast majority of cases. If the officer was behind the horse, he could not catch the animal, and if he were in front of it, he would have to put his own life at risk to stop it and would still likely be unsuccessful. The mounted police officer, however, could follow the runaway at full gallop, and gradually stop the frightened animal once he got alongside it. In such thoroughfares as Bedford Avenue and Flatbush Avenue hundreds of runaways were stopped and lives saved by the prompt action of the Mounted Squad.

The mounted policemen did much more than chase runaway horses. They performed the same duty as officers covering posts on foot but were in a much better position to respond quicker and for greater distances than the foot patrolman. Another benefit of the mounted officers that is still relevant today was their value in handling crowds.

There were numerous instances in which the Mounted Squad saved lives. On January 17th, 1881, Mrs. Emma Emmons and her little daughter were riding in a sleigh near Prospect Park. The horse pulling the sleigh became frightened and dashed off at full speed. Officer Watson, of the Mounted Squad, observed the runaway, and although quite a distance away he went into a full gallop and subdued the horse just before it ran into a group of trees. If it had made it into the trees, it would have smashed the sleigh to bits and likely killed the mother and child. The husband of the rescued woman and child presented Officer Watson, through General Jourdan, with an expensive gold medal.

On May 25th, 1877, Richard Lillie left his truck standing on Bedford Avenue with three small children aboard it. The team of horses attached to the truck took fright and ran off at full speed along the avenue. Officer Gustav Wessman, of the Mounted Squad, observed the occurrence and followed up at a gallop, stopping the horses and saving the children. For his heroic act Wessman was presented with a valuable silver medal.

Officer Wessman had the best record of any of the members of the Mounted Squad and was a fine horseman, but he eventually paid a price for his attention to duty. On July 13, 1877, he was galloping after a runaway when his horse tripped on a sunken switch and went down. Wessman sustained a broken arm and a head injury, but he fully recovered after several months and returned to duty. During December of 1877, while in the process of stopping a runaway horse, the wheel of the wagon struck Wessman's horse, knocking Wessman out of his saddle and seriously injuring him.[90] He was laid up for over a month and when he was ready to return to duty, General Jourdan assigned Wessman as the Harbor Master at Wallabout Basin. Wessman celebrated his new assignment by getting drunk and was arrested by two policemen from the Fourth Precinct before they realized he was a police officer. [91] A few days later Officer Wessman testified before Commissioner Jourdan and the case was dismissed, with Jourdan making his assignment as Harbor Master permanent.[92]

"ROUNDSMAN."

STOPPING A RUNAWAY.

THE SANITARY SQUAD

Around 1860, Brooklyn received a large influx of immigrants. Many brought with them a fear of government institutions and health facilities. At times they proved so serious an obstacle to the Board of Health, that the latter called upon the Metropolitan Board of Police, to detail a squad of men to preserve order and assist the Board of Health in their work of preventing and remedying disease. The squad was in such constant use that it became known as the Sanitary Squad and finally was detached and put under the sole control of the health authorities.

At one time it consisted of eight men and was frequently overworked in the discharge of its duties. Education, the appeals of press, and association with neighbors rapidly worked to change the opinions of these newcomers and to a large extent eradicated the problem. The work grew smaller, and the squad was reduced accordingly in size. With the re-organization of the police department, the squad was deprived of self-government and put under the joint control of the Central Office and the Board of Health. The routine work done by the Sanitary Squad became so insignificant that Sergeant Holbrook frequently detailed its members to duties belonging to the Central Office. There were times, however, when their best efforts were needed in aiding the physicians.

There were many new immigrants who were opposed to vaccination. When a case of smallpox broke out and the board -physicians were sent down to inoculate residents of the same building as they suffered, they would meet with violence at the hands of such people, were it not for the police escort.

    The attempts of the Board of Health to preserve the public health by cleaning out and disinfecting diseased buildings by ejecting the residents and condemning the building always produced intense excitement and rage in the displaced people. Without the Sanitary Squad to preserve the peace, a health - officer in such a case would be assaulted and possibly killed in the performance of his duty. As of 1887 the squad consisted of four officers but could be increased indefinitely in a few minutes upon request by the Board of Health upon the order of the chief of police.[93]

THE ROGUES GALLERY

Law enforcement technology continues to advance by leaps and bounds. It wasn't that long ago that facial recognition technology was the subject of science fiction novels. Facial recognition is here, but it is also controversial. Inclusion in a face recognition database means the face is always part of a lineup, and every time grainy surveillance footage surfaces of a robbery or assault, the suspect's face is being compared with millions of other unsuspecting faces.

The government has always sought a way to file away and compare the faces of the guilty, but until very recently the technology only allowed for it to occur in a much more rudimentary way. Before there was the fingerprint, or even the police file, there was the rogues' gallery, which was found in most U.S. police departments, including the City of Brooklyn. The gallery was a large wall or cabinet filled with photographs of alleged criminals that could be used as a way of identifying repeat offenders and coordinating surveillance, and as an example for witnesses. Police often scrawled on the back of the photographs a basic biographical sketch of the suspect, including known aliases and previous arrests. In many larger cities during the 1890s and early 1900s, the booking and photographing of an arrested person was also accompanied by the taking of Bertillon measurements. Developed in France, the system involved taking at least five specific bodily measurements including head length, foot length, and length of the middle finger. This data could be easily filed away and cross-referenced in case a suspect changed his appearance drastically. As cumbersome as this technology was, its use in the early 20th century posed the same ethical questions about guilt, innocence, and the nature of governance that we continue to grapple with on an exponentially larger scale.[94]

The Rogues' Gallery was one of the most important features of the Brooklyn Police Department in 1887. It was located in the detectives' room under the direction of Detective William D. Strong. It was not open to the public and could only be accessed by permission of the superintendent. The collection of photographs numbered over three thousand. All the pictures in the possession of the department taken prior to November 20, 1877, were kept in large albums, of which there were over a dozen, and those taken since that date were exhibited in a large cabinet. Attached to the cabinet were record books with numbers corresponding to those inscribed under each picture. These contained the name, age, record and disposition of cases and were kept in drawers in the lower part of the cabinet. Every grade of criminal from the murderer to the petty sneakthief had a photo in the collection.

The first picture in the cabinet was that of John Owens, a petty thief, who was sentenced to imprisonment for six months. Number one hundred and fifty - six was a picture that would naturally attract attention. It was that of John M. Wright, the murderer of old Barney Feron, the Red- Hook boatman. The photograph represented a light-haired youth, with good features, a low narrow forehead and a small nose and thin lips, the last person one would suspect of being a cold-blooded murderer.

The most repulsive features exhibited in the cabinet were those of William B. Dayton, number five hundred and twenty- nine, who was arrested for burglary and sentenced to imprisonment for one year. When the time came for Dayton to have his picture taken, the authorities found that they had a tough job on hand. He strenuously objected to undergo the operation and twisted and squirmed in every direction. An officer finally got hold of his ears and forced him down in the chair and held him while the photographer uncovered his camera. Dayton seeing that the photo had to be taken, determined that no one would recognize him by twisting his mouth and rolling up his eyes until nothing but the whites were visible.

The photograph, when finished, looked as much like the photographer as it did the thief, and Dayton was happy.

The disgrace associated with having one's picture in the Rogue's Gallery led to curious results. Unrepentant criminals recognized them as dangerous aids to the police when the latter were engaged in looking for the perpetrators of a crime. Reformed criminals regarded them as constant witnesses of their past life. Both classes desired to destroy or remove their portraits from the collection. The practice of the department in these cases was actuated as much by mercy as by justice. When a reformed criminal had shown by an honest life that he was truly a repentant man and satisfied the superintendent of the fact, the latter removed the portrait. Where a man has been unjustly accused and acquitted on the merits, or wrongfully convicted and afterwards pardoned, the same practice prevailed. Here the courts had jurisdiction and in several cases had commanded the removal or destruction of a photograph where the police had refused to comply with a request to that effect.[95]

HARBOR POLICE

On November 18, 1885, a great improvement was affected in the police administration of Brooklyn with the establishment of the same type of steamboat- squad that had been utilized by the New York authorities for many years. A boat was purchased by the city government and named "Judge Moore" in honor of the distinguished magistrate of the Court of Sessions.

The "Judge Moore" was a handsome vessel, half-tug and half steam yacht, forty feet long, eight beam, and three and one-half draught. Her build enabled her to steam rapidly, and at the same time safely handle the collisions, scrapings and concussions she met in prowling about the wharves and bulkheads and passing into crowded slips and basins. The vessel and crew, or squad, were attached to the Fifteenth Precinct and were nominally commanded by Captain Kellett. It took a daily rest at the foot of Atlantic Street, but nearly all the time, day and night, it was cruising along the waterfront, which extended from Newtown Creek at Hunter's Point, along the East River, Buttermilk Channel, New York Harbor and Gowanus Bay to the foot of Sixtieth Street at Bay Ridge.

The vessel usually got underway at 8 AM and returned at 4 PM, when the crew was changed. It then left again and returned after midnight. In summer it cruised all night. The "Judge Moore" did much more work than was usually believed. It pursued and captured river-pirates and recovered the booty, took part in saving life and property at fires on the riverfront or vessels, rescued drowning people, picked up derelict property, and intervened in quarrels between seamen, stevedores and other maritime and semi-maritime toilers. As a matter of fact, it only took a couple of days for the "Judge Moore" to see its first action.

As the patrol boat steamed up the river on the morning of November 20th, 1885 Officer Rodgers noticed two men unloading a quantity of sisal from a skiff at the foot of Degraw Street. Suspecting that they were river thieves, he gave the alarm and the little boat turned rapidly into the dock in which the thieves were at work. So quickly was this done that Officer Rodgers had leaped upon the dock and captured one of the men before they were aware of the patrol boat's presence. The other man ran when he saw what had happened but was soon apprehended. At the Fifteenth Precinct station house the men gave their names as Thomas Fitzgerald, 25-years-old, and James McGowan, 23-years-old. Over 400-pounds of sisal was recovered. [96]

The professional river thieves - the "Smoky Hollow" and "Red Hook Gangs," the "Canallers," the Gowanus and Bay Ridge gangs, the Eighth Ward "Hardscrabblers, " the Newtown and Wallabout crowds became things of the past. Before the steamboat squad was instituted it was a difficult task to apprehend the river thieves in the act. The moment they were discovered they took to the water, in which they were water rats and on which they were skilled and swift oarsmen. Beneath each wharf and in each bulkhead, were places, either left by the builders or constructed by the thieves, to which they would swim underwater and where they would remain for hours or until the police had gone away. The police boat changed all this, making the water more dangerous than the land for the criminals. As a consequence, the bolder crooks realized their occupation was gone and abandoned their long careers of piracy, and only the more contemptible class, the sneakthieves, remained. There was still a large element upon the waterfront which was required to be watched and kept under surveillance. Fortunately for Brooklyn, most of those areas were in New York.

A feature of the Brooklyn waterfront which was very noteworthy, was that it was nearly all under private and not public ownership. These owners were generally rich merchants or wealthy corporations, all of whom employed watchmen.

By 1887 the river thieves had declined significantly, but there were still some colorful characters on the water. One of the most notorious of the river pirates was Frank Schmidt, or, as he was more familiarly known, "Dutch Frank." For years he carried on his thieving operations without interruption. His exploits were of a most daring character, and his name became familiar with all vessel owners and consignees. The authorities tried every means in their power to capture him, but did not meet with success until the 13th of July 1885, when they caught him and placed him under lock and key. On the day of his arrest, "Dutch Frank," accompanied by Bernard and

Patrick Martin, two well -known dock thieves, visited the British steamship "Salisbury," which was then lying in the river at the foot of Pacific Street, and stole a hawser (a thick rope or cable for mooring or towing a ship) valued at fifty dollars. The Martin boys boarded the vessel and mingling with a crowd of visitors managed to secure the hawser and a quantity of rope, which they passed in the presence of the captain and crew over the side of the vessel to Schmidt, who had remained in a row-boat close to the stern. The captain, who was on deck at the time, saw the act, and as Schmidt rowed off called to the tugboat "James A. Garfield," which he boarded and immediately set chase for the fast-disappearing thief. Officer Martin Casey, in charge of the police patrol boat, the "Judge Moore," recognized "Dutch Frank," and getting up steam followed in the wake of the captain of the "Salisbury." Schmidt made for Governor's Island and landed about two minutes before his pursuers. He struck inland for a hiding place, but before he had gone a quarter of a mile was overtaken and after a short struggle made a prisoner. The "Judge Moore" took Schmidt back to Brooklyn, where he was arraigned before a Police Justice and remanded for an examination. He was finally taken before Judge Moore, in the Court of Sessions, but he was not immediately tried. While the case was pending, another charge of stealing two hundred and fifty dollars' worth of rope from the ship "Standard" was brought against him. This latter case came to trial, and Schmidt was found guilty and sent to prison for five years.

Even before the "Judge Moore," took to the river, it wasn't guaranteed that the thieves could get away as long as they stayed on the water. On May 29th, 1873, Joseph Gayles, alias "Socco the Bracer," "Bum" Mahoney, a first-class river-thief, and Billy Woods, formerly a stonecutter, stole a boat, and with muffled oars pulled down stream to a pier on the East River. They boarded the brig "Margaret," of New Orleans, and, while ransacking the captain's trunk, awakened the captain and mate. A scuffle ensued, which resulted in the thieves leaving the brig and taking to their boat. An alarm brought officers to the scene of the attempted robbery. It was three o'clock in the morning, the sky was overcast and not a star could be seen. As one of the officers flashed his dark lantern under the pier, he saw a boat starting out. Throwing the rays of his lantern full upon it, three men stood up, revolvers in hand, and firing began. The first shot gave "Socco" his death wound. The officers continued firing until they had emptied their pistols, but the thieves escaped in the darkness and pulled up toward the Long Island shore. "Socco the Bracer," fainted from the loss of blood, and his companions, thinking he was dead, threw him overboard to lighten the boat. The water revived him, and he begged piteously to be taken into the boat again. With much trouble and effort his partners were able to pull "Socco" on board, but as soon as he was on board he gasped and died. The boat was again stopped in mid-stream, and "Socco's" lifeless body was again thrown to the waters. Four days later "Socco" surfaced at the foot of Stanton Street, within sight of the residence of the dead river-thief. Secrecy was no longer possible, and now the thieves themselves admitted that their pal was killed by the officer. [97]

POLICE PARADE

From around 1857 until 1934 New York City maintained an annual tradition of holding a police parade. The purpose of the parade was to exhibit the military deportment, professionalism, equipment, and recent department innovations. A secondary purpose of the parade was to present medals earned by the members of the department through acts of heroism and valor performed during the prior year.

The police parade was only a distant memory when NYPD Commissioner Bill Bratton tried to revive the tradition. It was during the fall of 1994 that Bratton focused on preparing to celebrate the 150th anniversary of the NYPD the following October. He planned a ticker tape parade led by himself and Mayor Rudolph Giuliani. Giuliani had gone along with the idea until he discovered that the date Bratton had selected for the parade – Saturday, October 6th – happened to fall on Bratton's birthday. Interviewed on a television talk show, Bratton announced that he was going to have one of the biggest birthday celebrations in history. When Giuliani learned of the quote he had an aide inform Bratton that the parade was history.[98]

Brooklyn began its police parade tradition on Tuesday, May 18, 1887. At about two o'clock in the afternoon, five hundred and fifty uniformed officers of the Brooklyn Police force formed in line at the fountain on Bedford Avenue. It was the occasion of the first annual parade of the Brooklyn Police Department. Just prior to the word to march everything was in confusion. Policemen seemed to be everywhere, hurrying, scurrying here and there in the hot broiling sun. Strangers in town would have no doubt mistaken it for some riot, which the entire force of the city had been called upon to quell. To a person who lived in the city, however, the burnished helmets, polished buttons and clean uniforms told a different tale. Shortly after 2 PM, the word to march was given. As if by magic all noise ceased. The men were all in line and had started before many of the spectators who had left their points of vantage could regain them. In the lead was the mounted squad under the command of Sergeant Johnson. He presented a magnificent and imposing appearance. Their horses, with glossy hides and well combed manes, looked magnificent. The horses seemed to appreciate the thunderous applause from the excited and admiring host of spectators who lined each side of the street.

Following the horses came the drum corps of the Ninth Regiment of the New York State National Guard with Superintendent Campbell following in all the glory of a brand-new uniform. By his side marched Inspector Reilly, the head of the detective force of Brooklyn. After them came the 550 men of the department. They were divided into two battalions of nine companies each, with fourteen files full. The only captain not on parade was Captain Woglom, of the Fifth Precinct, for whom a walk of six miles was physically impossible. He was put on duty at headquarters and did all that the superintendent usually does when there.

A GLIMPSE OF THE MOUNTED SQUAD.

The men wore for the first time the new summer helmets, and every uniform was adjusted so carefully that even the eagle eye of the inspector could find no flaw or spot. The route was from the fountain through Bedford Avenue to Lafayette, through Lafayette to Schermerhorn Street, to Clinton, through Clinton to Remsen, and through Remsen to the City Hall, where they were reviewed by Mayor Whitney, Commissioner Carroll and Deputy Commissioner Dallon, who expressed themselves as extremely gratified at the display. No doubt the citizens felt so too, to think that such an imposing and efficient force guarded their interests. After passing the Hall they marched to Gallatin Place, Fulton Street, where they disbanded.

Although so large a force marched, all the posts were covered as usual, 254 men being left on guard, 190 of them being regulars and the remainder being called in from detailed positions.[99]

REVIEWED BY THE MAYOR FROM THE CITY HALL STEPS.

GLIMPSE OF THE POLICE PARADE ON BEDFORD AVENUE.

PENSION

When I joined the New York City Transit Police Department in 1981, one of the most attractive aspects of the job was the pension. I could work twenty years and then reap the benefits of a half pay pension for the rest of my life. So far, I've received more than $1 million in pension payments from the City of New York, and I hope I'm around to receive another million.

Police pensions weren't always that generous. As a matter of fact, they rarely existed until the latter part of the 19th century. In Brooklyn, an act to create a police pension fund for disabled and retired policemen in the city was passed, on June 15th, 1877. The act stipulated that the pensions be funded as follows:

First - The capital, income, interest, dividends, cash, deposits, securities and credits, now belonging to said police life insurance fund with the addition thereto, from time to time, of

Second - Twenty per centum of all moneys paid into the treasury of excise for licenses.

Third - All fines imposed by the Commissioners of Police and Excise upon the members of the police force, and,

Fourth - All rewards, gifts, fees, testimonials and emoluments that may be presented, paid or given to any member of the police on account of police service, except such as shall be allowed by the Commissioner of Police and Excise to be retained by said members, and,

Fifth - All lost or stolen moneys remaining in the hands of the property clerk for the space of one year, and for which there shall be no lawful claimant, and moneys arising from the sale by said property clerk of unclaimed property; and,

Sixth - A sum of money equal to fifty cents per month for each member of the police force and attaché of the police department, to be paid monthly by the comptroller of the city to the treasurer of the board of trustees of the police pension fund from money deducted from the pay of members and attaches of said force on account of lost time;

Seventh - the sum of three dollars per day, or for any portion of a day, for each member of the police force or attaché of the police department, whose services may be required by any corporation, association, person or persons, whatever, for performance of any police duty (except in criminal cases) outside of the city of Brooklyn which sum in each and every case shall be paid to the treasurer of the board of trustees of the police pension fund for the benefit of said fund. The Board of Estimates of the city of Brooklyn is authorized and directed from time to time, by resolution of said board, to a propriate from the excise moneys derived by the Commissioners of Excise from licenses' for the sale of intoxicating liquors, twenty per centum of the moneys so derived, and the comptroller of said city shall draw his warrant in favor of the trustees of said pension fund, and the treasurer of said city shall pay such warrants out of the said moneys received for said licenses.

Eighth - A sum of money, equal to, but not greater than one per centum of the monthly pay, salary or compensation of each member of the police force, to be deducted monthly by the comptroller of the city from the pay, salary or compensation of each and every member of the police force, and the said comptroller is authorized, empowered and directed to deduct said sum of money as aforesaid and forthwith to pay the same to the treasurer of the police pension fund provided, however, that any attaché of the said police department, who, at the time of the passage of the act, shall have served seven years and upwards upon the said police force shall be entitled to the benefits of the provisions of this act upon payment by him of a sum of money equal to one per centum of the monthly pay , salary or compensation of the said attaché, as hereinafter provided for in the case of members of the police force. All the moneys derived from sources mentioned in this section shall be paid over by the officers and persons having the collection or custody of the same to the trustees of the said police a pension fund and shall belong to and be invested as portions of said fund.

The Board of Police and Excise have the power to grant pensions to any member of the police force or attaché of the police department from moneys from the Pension Fund, to be paid by the Board of Trustees as follows:

(1) To the widow of any member of the police force or attaché of the department who shall have been killed while in actual performance of police duty, or shall have died from the effects of any injuries received whilst in the actual discharge of such duty, or who has died after ten years' service in the police department, provided such death shall not have been caused by misconduct on his part, a sum not to exceed three hundred dollars per annum.

(2) To any child or children under eighteen years of age of such member of the police force, killed or dying as aforesaid, but leaving no widow; if a

widow, then after her death, to such child or children being yet under the age of eighteen years, such pension as the Board of Pension and Excise shall from time to time award and order, not to exceed three hundred dollars per annum.

(3) To any such member of the police force or attaché of the department, who, whilst in the actual performance of police duty, and by reason of the performance of said duty, and without fault and misconduct on his part, shall have become permanently disabled, physically or mentally, so as to be unfitted to perform full police duty, a sum not to exceed three hundred dollars per annum.

(4) To any member of the police force or attaché of the department who shall, after ten years' membership, become superannuated by age or rendered incapable of performing full police duty by reason of disability or disease contracted without misconduct on his part, a sum not to exceed three hundred dollars.

(5) To any such member of the police force or attaché of the department who shall, after fifteen years' membership, become superannuated by age or rendered incapable of performing full police duty by reason of disability or disease, four hundred dollars per annum.

(6) Any member of the force or attaché of the department who has or who shall have performed police duty for a period of twenty years or upwards shall, upon his own application in writing, be retired from service and placed on the police pension roll, and thereupon pay shall be awarded, granted and paid from said Police Pension Fund, by the trustees thereof, an annual sum during his lifetime equal to one -half the full member of said police force of the rank of the member so retired, provided, however, that no pension so granted shall exceed the sum of one thousand dollars per annum.

(7) In every case mentioned in subdivisions three, four and five of section four of this act, the Board of Police and Excise shall determine the circumstances thereof in its discretion, and may order the retirement from service and payment of the pensions mentioned in this act, but only after the certificates and recommendations of the surgeons in writing shall be on file, as required by the provisions of this act, under such rules and regulations as they may prescribe, but all payments on account of said Police Pension Fund shall be made quarterly, by check or draft upon the trustees of said sum, signed as said trustees may direct.

Pensions to widows shall terminate when the widow shall remarry; and pensions to children shall terminate whenever the children shall respectively arrive at the age of eighteen years. The Board of Police and Excise may, in its discretion, order any pensions granted or any part thereof to cease, except to members of the police force or attachés retired after twenty years' service, as provided in section five of the act, but in all such cases the said Board of Police and Excise shall file with the trustees-of the police pension fund a written statement of the cause which determined them in ordering such pension to cease, and nothing herein or in any other act contained shall render the granting or payment of such pension obligatory on the Board of Police and Excise, or upon the trustees of the police pension fund or charge able as a matter of right upon said police pension fund, except as provided in section five of this act.

No member of the police force or attaché of the police department, shall be awarded, granted or paid a pension on account of physical or mental disability or disease, unless upon the certificate and recommendation of the Board of Surgeons of the Department of Police, which shall set forth in detail the cause, nature and extent of the disability, disease or injury of each member of the police force, or attaché of said police department who may be placed upon the pension roll, and said certificate shall distinctly state whether or not such disability, disease or injury was incurred or sustained by said member of the police force or attaché in the performance of police duty and without misconduct on his part, and such certificate shall in each case be filed with and entered upon the minutes of the trustees of the Police Pension Fund.

In 1877 the Legislature passed an act giving fifty per cent. of the dog tax to the Pension Fund. The dog tax amounted to $ 2.50 for each dog, to be paid by the owner of said dog, and as there were about ten thousand dogs in the city, made the full tax about $ 25,000, half of which, $ 12,500, went into the Pension Fund. In 1877 the fund had on its roll one hundred and fifty-seven pensioners.[99]

POLICE MATRONS

Marie Owens is not a familiar name to most Americans, but she was an important pioneer. In 1890 Miss Owens became the first female police officer when she was appointed to the Chicago Police Department. Although there were no female police officers in Brooklyn at that time, three years before Owens was sworn in the Brooklyn Police Department did bring females into the department to perform a different function.

At a meeting of the Board of Aldermen on May 24th, 1887, the Committee on Police and Excise reported resolutions appointing a number of Police Matrons. The committee in its report noted that a committee of the Kings County Woman's Association stated that women and girls were brought into court charged with crimes of which they were innocent. They cited a case where a young girl was arrested and charged with the crime of larceny. When the case was investigated it was found that the girl was innocent, and that the charge was made for the purpose of preventing her leaving the family where she was employed. The conclusion of the committee was that females would be an invaluable in determining if these females were being falsely accused.

The Police Matron system was adopted in Portland, and subsequently in Boston and Philadelphia, before being put in operation in Brooklyn. The program was successful in assisting a large number of women to lead useful and productive lives, who otherwise may have been placed in prison. The Matron Program was adopted so that women and girls brought into court (many for the first time) charged with misdemeanors, should have the presence and assistance of a person of their own sex, in an official capacity, to whom they could turn.

Besides assisting women under arrest, Matrons were valuable when it came to dealing with "Little Wanderers," – small children who wandered away from home or a parade and became lost. When they were picked up by police they were placed under the care of these matrons. They seldom knew where they lived, and frequently a youngster, just big enough to go out alone, was found two or three miles away from home, having escaped the dangers of street crossings and car tracks in some unaccountable way. When the distracted mother came, there was always a scene. It was a happy scene if the child was with the matron inside the station house, but if the frantic mother was reporting her child missing, the matron was still a valuable resource in calming and reassuring the frightened parent.[100]

THE FIRE THREAT

During the nineteenth century, fire was perhaps the most severe environmental threat faced by Americans, especially in urban areas. Before the Civil War, hundreds of large fires destroyed property worth over 200 million dollars in the nation's principal cities. After 1865, conflagrations routinely destroyed large parts of cities. Brooklyn was no exception.[101]

On December 5th, 1876, nearly one thousand playgoers entered the Brooklyn Theatre, at Washington and Johnson Streets near City Hall, to enjoy the well-reviewed production of "The Two Orphans."

During the show's final act, stagehands discovered that a set piece backstage had caught fire. The actors onstage attempted gamely to stay in character, for fear of causing panic, until fiery bits of wood and flaming parts of the set began raining down upon them.

As the audience leapt to the aisles in terror, the actors tried to calm people to prevent a stampede, to no avail. An usher forced open a rarely used exit door to free audience members, but the rush of December air only fed the flames, turning the once elegant auditorium, built only five years previous, into an inescapable trap of heat and asphyxiation. Those in the top tiers of the theatre – the "cheap seats" filled with men, women, and children – were trapped by smoke within darkened foyers and unnavigable stairwells. Some fell from balconies to their deaths. Dozens were crushed heading for doorways, and to some of those who survived, it seemed that all respectability had given way to base animal behavior. Most perished by suffocation or underfoot, while others were lost in the choking smoke. Flaming projectiles caught in the wind settled upon surrounding structures, and firefighters scrambled to soak the inferno, now in fear of scattering randomly through the neighborhood.

Since 1869, Brooklyn had a paid fire department, and many fought the blaze from the street. But the rudimentary firefighting implements of the day were unable to combat the inferno. Fire Chief Nevins said that when he arrived at the fire, engines 5, 6, and 7 were already at work, along with trick 2. He said that for some time the police were not able to maintain any semblance or order, as they not only had to assist ladies and children who were separated, but they also had to look to the safety of the First Precinct station house, which was dangerously close to the fire.[102] The Brooklyn Theatre burned for several hours more, dying out by early morning. Throughout the night, most could only watch, and many did watch. Thousands flocked to the scene, some to help, others just fascinated and horrified.

The scene outside the burning theater was chaotic. Before daylight it was found necessary to reinforce the police officers charged with keeping the approaches to the theatre clear of curiosity seekers. There seemed to be no abatement of the public curiosity to inspect the ruins. It was in some instances so intrusive that the police were compelled to use force to keep back the crowd, as all sorts of stories and excuses were used to get through the police lines.

Captain Smith, of the First Precinct, was on duty for almost 36- consecutive hours before going home for a few hours of much needed rest. Inspector Waddy assumed charge of the First Precinct during Captain Smith's absence. Inspector Waddy set up a system of passes which were issued to friends and relatives searching for loved ones at the locations bodies had been taken. Among the first to apply for a pass was a grief-stricken woman, who in broken English, stated her son, a young man of twenty-five, had gone to the theater and had been missing since. Inspector Waddy handed her a pass as she sobbed. Similar cases were constantly occurring, and upwards of two

hundred passes were granted by Inspector Waddy alone.
Captain Smith was in possession of all sorts of articles
from a gold stud to a seal skin saque. In the yard of the
stationhouse lay the bodies of actors Burroughs and
Mirdoch, as a group of actors stood by mournfully
discussing the manner of their deaths

The scene was too much for the police to control, so
the New York State National Guard was requested.
Colonel McLeer established his headquarters at the City
Hall, in the Pension Office. The Colonel reported to Chief
of Police Campbell, who directed Colonel McLeer to take
orders from Inspector Waddy at the First Precinct.[103]
Inspectors found an unspeakably grisly sight the
next morning, heaps of burned bodies in formless masses –
people choked or crushed, their remains almost

unrecognizable amid blackened debris. A make-shift morgue was prepared on nearby Adams Street to accommodate the dozens of unidentified corpses.[104]

The scene at the makeshift Adams Street morgue was becoming uncontrollable, requiring Colonel McLeer to send forty men to the site to keep the crowd in check.[105] The crowds continued to grow as the remains of 91-people were brought to the morgue, and all but thirteen were recognized and removed by family and friends. The police eventually had the makeshift morgue running like clockwork. Detective Riggs had charge of the room where the majority of bodies were placed, and on the outside of the building police maintained order under the command of Sergeant Strong. All the bodies were stretched out on the floor of the room, situated on the west side of the building, and people who obtained a pass were admitted through this room in singe file by the police. All the unidentified bodies were placed near the door.[106]

Much of the responsibility for the efficient police operations in the chaotic environment fell to the staff of the Police Property Clerk. William H. Muldoon, a former newspaperman, was the Property Clerk, and it was his office's responsibility to maintain all the property that came into the possession of the police department. His role after the fire was extremely critical because many of the bodies were burned beyond recognition, and the only way some identifications were made was based on the property found on the bodies.

Nobody is exactly sure how many died that evening – some number between 275 and 300 people. The place where the theater once stood is now occupied by Cadman Plaza, in the grove of trees just east of the Henry Ward Beecher statue. Many of the bodies are buried together under a memorial at Green-Wood Cemetery.

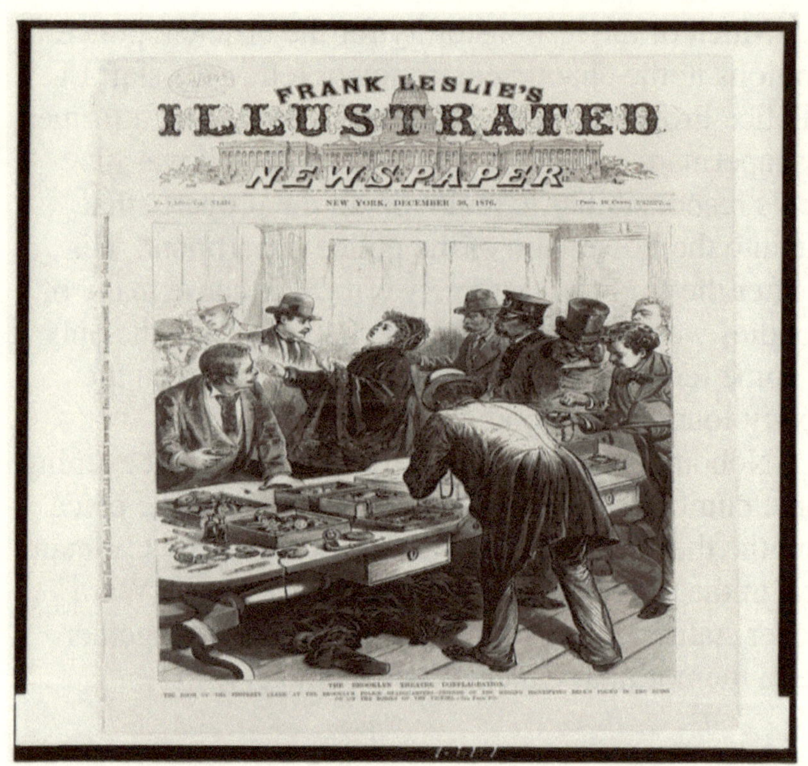

Property Clerk personnel work with property recovered from the fire

The makeshift morgue on Adams Street

The theatre fire was not the only harrowing experience Muldoon would face as Property Clerk. In April 1887 he received a beating while he worked in the Property Clerk Office in the Municipal Building. The assault was not by some drunken thug who snuck into the building. Muldoon received his thrashing from the "Keeper of City Hall."

The Keeper of City Hall was a position appointed by the mayor whose duties made the job sound something like the janitor of the building. Jim Dunne, a former prizefighter, was the Keeper of City Hall. In 1887 prizefighting was mostly illegal in Brooklyn. Muldoon wrote an article which appeared in a newspaper urging the city not to license prizefighting and referring to most prizefighters as being less than model citizens. The article pointed out Jim Dunne as an example of a degenerate prizefighter and alluded to his responsibility in the death of Jim Elliot, another prizefighter.

Muldoon was calmly conversing with Inspector Mackellar in the Property Clerk Office when Dunne burst in and grabbed Muldoon by his collar.

"Are you trying to get square on me?" Dunne growled.

"What do you mean?" asked Muldoon.

"Didn't you write the article yesterday morning?" Dunne said, while maintaining his grip on Muldoon.

"What article?" Muldoon gasped.

"You know what I mean," Dunne responded, "and I'm gonna lick you right here, right now."

Dunne tossed Muldoon from one side of the room to the other. All Muldoon could do was cover up his face in the corner while Dunne hit him with body blows while looking for an opening to the face.

"Don't do this to me," Muldoon pled.

"I'm gonna lick you anyway," Dunne said as he threw Muldoon to the floor. Dunne lifted his foot and prepared to stomp Muldoon when Inspector Mackellar grabbed Dunne on his shoulder. Dunne did not continue his kick, but instead spun around and punched MacKellar in the mouth, cutting his lower lip. Muldoon took the opportunity to get up and run from the office with Dunne in hot pursuit. He ran down the corridor towards the Commissioner's office where Police Officer George Rogers tried to stop him, but Dunne tossed him aside like a child. Deputy Commissioner Dallon also failed to stop Dunne. Finally, at the direction of Inspector Mackellar, Captain Folk and Captain French were able to calm Dunne.

Inspector Mackellar directed French and Folk to place Dunne under arrest. Turning to Mackellar, Dunne said, "You're a God damn fine policeman, you are. You're a disgrace to the force."

Dunne said he would not be placed under arrest by Captain Folk, but that he would let Captain French arrest him. "I'll go with you. You're a God damn nice democrat."

In a commentary to the politics of the era, Jim Dunne was fined $250, which he puled out of his pocket and paid immediately. He also was able to keep his job as the Keeper of City Hall.[107]

The threat of fire increased in 1877 in the form of the new, but potentially deadly kerosene lamp. The new burning fluid had become universally popular with the convenience outshining the dangers and a misplaced overconfidence possessed by many who felt they knew how to handle the lamps safely. As a result, the reckless or ignorant would fill lamps with kerosene in the immediate vicinity of a flame, kindle fires with it, and even brighten up fires that were in full combustion. There were also almost no legal restrictions placed upon the manufacture or sale of kerosene allowing dishonest merchants to put vast quantities of the oil on the market that were so impure that they were in reality a form of liquid gunpowder.

Eight persons were killed, fifty injured, and over 250-fires were cause by the reckless use of kerosene or the use of impure oils in 1877 alone. The increased workload thrust upon the police resulted in the passage and enforcement of laws and ordinances whereby manufacturers and dealers were forbidden from selling illuminating oils that was not tested to a specified temperature level, and all retailers had to obtain a license for the purpose of selling kerosene.

These changes, which were chiefly due to General James Jourdan, led to the creation of the Bureau of Combustibles, which was responsible for dealing with the kerosene issues. This relieved the police department from managing the kerosene problem and effectively closed what was call the "kerosene period" in Brooklyn history.

Even with the Bureau of Combustible and the paid Fire Department, the Police Department always had a role as a first responder during fires. In 1882 Patrolman William Knipe, of the Fourth Precinct was on patrol at 3:40 AM when he observed smoke coming from the second story of 142 Grand Avenue. He immediately ran to the location, entered through the front door and ran upstairs. The smoke was so thick that it drove him back down to the first floor where he helped Mrs. Bridget Whelehan out to the street. Officer Knipe made another attempt to reach the second floor but was again driven back by the smoke. He returned to the sidewalk where a small boy told him there were children on the second floor. Knipe again attempted to make it to the second floor. This time he could hear a man's voice pleading for help. The fire was burning so fiercely that he could not enter the room, so he retuned to the sidewalk in time to see Mr. John Loftus appear at the second floor window. Loftus proceeded to throw his six children out the window with Officer Knipe catching each child. He then assisted Loftus and his wife out the window, which was ten feet above the sidewalk. The only injury sustained was a slight scorching of Officer Knipe's moustache.

The cause of the fire was determined to be an explosion of kerosene in a lamp in Bridget Whelehan's apartment.

BEYOND POLICEWORK

Not all the activities of the Brooklyn Police Department involved police work. The game of baseball has been America's pastime for a long time, with reporters describing baseball as a mania as far back as the 1840s. The sport was already established as a popular pastime when Civil War soldiers on both sides played it as a diversion. Many veterans took the game home after the war, and it became a great unifier in the years that followed the bloodiest conflict in U.S. history.

Mention baseball in Brooklyn and people will blurt "Dodgers," even though it's been many decades since "Dem Bums" thrilled the fans and broke their hearts at Ebbets Field. It was back in 1883 that the team currently known as the Dodgers was formed. The name Brooklyn Trolley Dodgers was first used to describe the team in 1895. The Dodgers, or Trolley Dodgers, were not the only baseball team in Brooklyn receiving attention in the Brooklyn newspapers in the latter part of the 19th century. Several amateur clubs received coverage right alongside the Dodgers including the Brooklyn Police Department Baseball Team. I was amazed at the depth and scope of the newspaper coverage given to Brooklyn police baseball. As a matter of fact, in 1887 almost a full page was devoted to profiling the starting lineup of the police squad in the type of article one might see in today's New York papers on opening day detailing the Yankees or Mets. Here is the comprehensive article that appeared in the May 28th, 1887 edition of the Brooklyn Times Union that provided a detailed scouting report of the Brooklyn Police Baseball Team.

BROOKLYN'S POLICE NINE – MEN WHO WILL WEILD THE ASH ON THE BALL FIELD – Stronger this year than ever before and well uniformed and equipped - ready to meet the representatives of the Finest from New York and confident of victory.

In the Police Department of Brooklyn athletic sports, highest among which may be counted the national game of baseball, have never received the encouragement that they have in some other cities that may be mentioned, and yet a more athletic set of men than the police force of this city constitute it would be difficult to find. New York has its baseball nine and so does Brooklyn, yet among the men there is this great difference, that in the city across the river the members of the nine are excused from duty when they have any legitimate game on hand, while here they have to take their own time or else place themselves under obligations to their superior officers and get their associates to stand their tours of duty while they play. It cannot be said that the fault lies with any of the officials at Headquarters, for the police force of Brooklyn is rather inadequate, and it is many times impossible to allow an afternoon off, however advantageous a game of baseball would be, both physically and mentally. Yet the police officials take great interest in Brooklyn's baseball nine, and they crow in delight at victories in the same proportion that they feel gloomy in defeat.

None of the gentleman connected with the Central Office takes a greater interest in the police baseball nine than Thomas Carroll Jr., the son of the Commissioner. Mr. Carroll is about 26-years of age, and he still retains all the interest in the national game that he had when a boy. His official position in the department is accountant, but the members of the nine speak of him as "Our Manager," and they use the term with the greatest pride. Mr. Carroll uses a portion of his time when not engaged with startling rows of figures and reports from precincts in laying plans to ensure the success of the nine in the games it is expected to play during the season. His interest in it is shown in more than one practical way, but which will be most noticeable on the field will be the new uniforms he has provided. Heretofore the club has been arrayed in borrowed uniforms, but Mr. Carroll's generosity has now provided it so that it will have to beg of no organization for the means of making a decent field appearance. The new uniform consists of blue shirts, knickerbockers and caps, with red stockings and belts and the words "BROOKLYN POLICE" across the front of the shirts in red letters. That the boys when on the field will look as well as the next and that they will do themselves proud goes without saying to those who know what a set of good looking muscular young men they are.

The field captain of the club is M.J. Finnegan, who covers all the ground around second base in a style that would make the great Buck Ewing envious. Patrolman Finnegan did more than any other man to organize the police nine, and he has kept it with a solid front for many seasons past, arranging the games to be played and aiding greatly in winning the majority of them too. He sports a moustache that rivals that of the great Lawyer O'Rourke, of the New York nine and he performs his part in a game with just as much vim as that noted player does. He is an old-time baseball enthusiast, and his name may be found on many records during the palmy days from '73 to '76. He was catcher for the Marion club in 1873, and in 1874 and 1875 he played on the Reliance team. He went to the semi-professional Atlantics in 1876, but at the end of the season he dropped the ash to take up the locust, being in the early part of 1877 appointed upon the police force. Mr.

Finnegan was born in Brooklyn in 1854. He is now attached to the Fifth Precinct under command of Captain Woglom and wears his two stripes like a thorough policeman.

John Raleigh, of the Third Precinct, is the pitcher for the nine and he twirls the ball in a way that is bewildering to the batsman. He was a ball player way back in the days of 1875 when he pitched for the Hudson Club, a South Brooklyn organization. He was so well thought of then that he retained the same position during the seasons of 1876, 1877, and 1878, and then he transferred his affections and his skill to the well-known Flyaway Club, with which he played during 1879. After that, other duties called him away from regular attendance upon the diamond, but he has always held an enthusiastic interest in the game.

The nine is fortunate at having at the tall end of its battery a catcher, who thoroughly understands the pitcher. The occupant of this important place is James C. Raleigh, also of the Third Precinct. A record of his history as a baseball player is simply a repetition of that of his brother, John Raleigh. He caught or occupied third base for the Hudson Club from 1875 to 1878, and then, he too went to the Flyaway Club, for which during 2nd base in 1879.

The position of first baseman on the nine will be played by George Golden of the Thirteenth Precinct, who, when occasion demands, can also put on the gloves and mask and occupy the place behind the bat. Golden first played ball in Poughkeepsie with the Volunteers Club. That was just ten years ago. Then he went to Oswego where he was attached to the nine bearing the name of the town. For the next three years he followed the fortunes of the game with several local clubs, and 1882 found him

doing good work for the Allegheny Club of Pittsburgh, Pa.
He was appointed upon the police force in 1884, and
during the past two seasons he has played with the police
nine. He is 28 years old.

Joseph E. Farrell, of the Third Precinct, will look
after the interests of the nine at third base. He is another
offshoot from the Hudson Club, with which he began
playing in 1874, filling the catcher's place and other
positions. While he was with the Hudson's in 1876, that
club won the amateur championship pennant from the
Nameless, Winous, Osceola and other clubs.   He began
the season of 1877 with the Brooklyn Club. They only
played twelve games before they disbanded, but all of
them were victories. The New Bedford's, the Resolutes of
Elizabeth, the Princeton College, and other strong nines all
suffered defeat at their hands. With Bobby Matthews, now
of the Athletics of Philadelphia, and McGlynn, he joined
the Worcester Club and remained with them until they
consolidated with the Live Oak Club, of Lynn, Mass.
Then he returned to his first love the Hudson Club, and in
1878 aided them in winning the inter-state championship

from the Flyaway, Witoka, Orange, Astor, Montgomery and New York nines. In 1879 he played part of the season with the Hudson Club and the remainder with the Flyaway Club. He is 30 years old.

William Alnwick, who has been on the police force since 1885, will make his first appearance on the ball field with the police nine this season. He will act in the rather difficult position of shortstop, and if rumor be true in this instance, he will be a forceful addition both as concerns fielding and batting strength. Alnwick has not had the extended experiences on the diamond that some of the other players in the club have had, but he is a baseball man for all that. He was with the Monroe's in 1878 and 1879, and after taking a vacation from the pastime for several years he played with the Lily nine in 1883. Like the captain of the club, he is attached to the Fifth Precinct.

ALNWICK, S. S.

Richard Sandslands, of the Thirteenth Precinct, will look after the balls that fall into the right garden. He is an experienced player, having served with the police nine during the two seasons of 1885 and 1886. In 1877 he played with the successful Jackson Club in this city, and after that with other local nines. He was made a policeman in 1882 and is now 30 years old.

SANDLANDS, R. F.

George Clingman of the Twelfth Precinct is the tenth man on the team. He is a thorough all-around player and is expected to take the place of any man on the regular nine who on account of duty or other reasons will be ready to play. He played with the Amity Club in 1880 and 1881, and the next year became a member of the police force.

The left fielder of the nine will be Thomas Gallagher. This young man used to be an athlete of prominence and gained such distinction as a runner that his fellow athletes gave him the name of "Smoke," a title that speaks with eloquence for itself. Gallagher graduated from the Jefferson Club, for which he did good service during 1881 and 1882. He was appointed to the police force in 1883, but his professional duties still left him time to think of the national game, and he played on the police nine last year. He is a good batter, but those who know him best say he becomes weak in the legs after reaching first base and appears to have a greater inclination to sit on the bag than to try to steal to second. Captain Finnegan, however, has great faith in Gallagher. He is attached to the Fifth

Precinct, and his fellow officers say that his talents for practical joking – when off duty, of course, are tremendous.

Robert Allison will play in center field on the nine. He comes of an old baseball family, the name obtaining prominence through the efforts of "Andy" Allison, who was one of the reliables in the Eckford Club when it was in its palmiest days; when the Unions of Morrisania, the Haymakers of Troy, the Athletics of Philadelphia, the Mutuals of New York, and the Atlantics of Brooklyn, struggled for the championship, and when knickerbocker trousers were unknown upon the ball field. Robert Allison gained much of his baseball education on the Nameless Club, which won the amateur championship at Prospect Park on more than one occasion, and the Jefferson Club, with which he played in 1882. He was appointed upon the police force in 1883 and played on the police nine last year. He can pitch when necessary. He is now attached to the Sixth Sub-Precinct.

Taken as a body the Brooklyn Police nine should this year prove stronger than at any time previously. Their great drawback is the lack of advantage to practice together. They propose during the season to play games with the New York police nine, with which they now stand on even terms, with the Fire Department nine, should one be organized, with the police reporters and others. Last year they were on even terms as regards games won and lost with both the New Yorkers and the reporters.[108]

I found it fascinating how much press coverage was given to the Brooklyn Police team. In reading the article I also realized that the more things change the more they remain the same. I can relate to the complaint of the Brooklyn players mentioned in the article. They lamented that the New York Police team was given time off for their games while the Brooklyn policemen had to use their own time to play and sometimes could not be excused for a game.

I began my career with the NYC Transit Police and after the merger in 1995 I became a member of the NYPD. During my career I played with both the Transit Police Headquarters softball team and the NYPD Police Academy team. These were both championship caliber teams, and I never had a problem getting time off to play for one of these teams. Those playing on transit district or NYPD precinct teams were not as fortunate with receiving the time to play the games. As a matter of fact, I found two articles where the baseball team's games were affected by their police duties. The article notes how the team was compelled to suspend playing for a few weeks because of schedule changes to some of the players.[109]

I learned something else of importance regarding the Brooklyn Police Department through baseball via a 1904 article - six years after the Brooklyn Police Department ceased to exist after the Consolidation of Greater New York in 1898. The article referred to the Brooklyn/Queens Baseball team, indicating that years after the formation of the consolidated New York City Police Department, the Brooklyn Police still maintained an identity. This made sense, and again, I can relate to the concept of department identity during my experience with the merger of the Transit Police into the NYPD in 1995. The day of the merger the only things that changed were the uniform patch I wore and the shield I carried. Everything else essentially remained the same. I still worked in a transit district, only now it was part of the NYPD Transit Bureau instead of the Transit Police Department. The public and press still called us transit cops and transit policing on the subway remained the same. I would venture to guess that a very similar situation developed for the Brooklyn Police after 1898. The policemen working in a Brooklyn precinct continued working the same posts in the same neighborhoods, the only difference being that the precincts were renumbered.

The baseball team was just one example of how there was still a Brooklyn Police identity long after the consolidation. How long did this Brooklyn identity remain? I'm not certain, but again I'll relate to my experience as a transit cop. The Transit Police Department ceased to exist as an organization almost thirty years ago. There are still a few active members of the NYPD who began their careers as transit cops and who keep the memory of the Transit Police Department very much alive. As the last of these original transit cops retire the memory of the Transit Police Department is likely to fade with them. I would think it was the same in the early years of the 20th century. As long as there were policemen who worked for the Brooklyn Police Department active on the NYPD, the Brooklyn Police maintained an identity. Once the Brooklyn officers retired it would only be a few more years before the identity of the Brooklyn Police Department faded away with them.

Politics played a big part in the Brooklyn Police Department of the late 19th century, and that included baseball. First, I have to clarify that it appeared that there was one department team but there was also inter-department competition between precinct teams. Naturally, the players on the precinct teams were supposed to work in the precinct they were playing for, but the desire to win sometimes tempted teams to cut corners. Such was the case in 1895 when Captain French took the baseball squad from his precinct to play a game against a team from the Twenty-First Precinct managed by Police Officer Oscar Jones. Before the game commenced,

Captain French's team accused the Twenty-First Precinct squad of using "ringers," as they accused several members of the team of being United States Marines. Captain French said his team would play against any members of the Twenty-First Precinct, but not against the Marines. He took his team off the field and departed, directing Officer Jones to contact him when they could field a team of all policemen.[110]

Even though baseball was an amateur endeavor for the police, since they were representing the Brooklyn Police Department on the field, they still had to receive permission to form a team. For example, in May of 1888, Detective Michael Finnegan, the captain of the police team, had to request permission from Commissioner Bell for the police team to play in 1888. This was the Commissioner's response:

May 9, 1888

Detective Michael Finnegan:

My Dear Sir: In reply to yours in the 8th instant, just received, I have to say that you have my full authorization to go on in the usual way and organize your baseball nine. The only instruction I have to give on the subject is that you should organize a good nine, so that you can be able to defeat all comers.

I think I will be able to find time to be present on some occasion when your nine play. I have the honor to remain very truly yours,

J.D. Bell: Commissioner of Police and Excise [111]

Who exactly did the Brooklyn Police baseball team compete against? In 1890 I found an article documenting a game against the Brooklyn Fire Department. The game was held in Ridgewood Park to commemorate the reunion of the War Veterans of Kings County on July 15th, 1890.

The police defeated the firemen 16 to 5 and were awarded the Grand Army of the Republic Trophy which was displayed at police headquarters.

Another Police victory in 1889 was covered in such detail in the Brooklyn Citizen that the story covered almost two full pages. Why would the newspaper recap every inning and every hit in this game? Suddenly, the reason for the in-depth coverage became crystal clear. The police won the game 15 to 8 against a team of reporters from the Brooklyn Citizen newspaper. The newspaper was covering a game involving its own employees.[112]

Remember how I mentioned the Brooklyn Police identity. This next game is a prime example. In another 1904 article the headline reads, BROOKLYN POLICE WIN. Six years after the Brooklyn Police Department was consolidated into the NYPD there was still a Brooklyn Police Baseball team. This particular game was played against a team called the Saratogas, and was not without controversy. The police won the game 20 to 6, but the Saratogas claimed that they lost because the umpire exhibited favoritism toward the police. 20 to 6? With a score like that I think the cops could have done well without any help from the umpire.[113]

Not every game for the police team was a success. In 1889, an article reported a loss to the New York Fire Department. The strange thing about this article was how little information it contained. The article stated that the police team lost, but it never mentioned the score. It noted that the game was played at the Polo Grounds, and that "Cooney," the pitcher for the police, was not very pleased – that's it.[114]

The greatest rivalry for the Brooklyn team was with the New York team. On September 13, 1888, Brooklyn defeated the New York Police 9-5 in ten innings in a game that was most remarkable for the 23-errors committed.

A final note on baseball, that was more a reference to baseball rather than a story about the Brooklyn Police team. On July 8th, 1904, a newspaper article appeared regarding Patrolman Joseph Fritz. The headline of the article read, ONE-LEGGED BEGGARS THIS "COP'S" SPECIALTY. The article was an unflattering story that alleged Officer Fritz spent most of his time arresting vagrant beggars, and that in two instances the beggars only had one leg. The story was very sarcastic in stating when Fritz observed one of the one-legged vagrants begging, he chased him, but even though Fritz was the pitcher on the police baseball team, it took him seven blocks to catch the one-legged man. Once caught, the beggar kicked Fritz with his wooden leg resulting in splinters in Fritz' leg.[115]

As profiled within the pages of the Brooklyn newspapers, the police baseball team fielded some very accomplished athletes. The most accomplished athlete on the force was not part of the baseball team, however. His Name was Nicholas Dunne.

Dunne was born in Kilkenny Ireland in 1862 and was appointed a patrolman with the Brooklyn Police Department in 1888. In 1892, the 5-foot 5-inch, 155-pound 30-year-old was assigned to the Twelfth Precinct. Dunne was an outstanding runner and had been a member of the National Athletic Club for several years. He didn't drink, smoke, or chew tobacco, and Dr. Sullivan, a police surgeon said Dunne possessed a pair of lungs as strong as any horse.
It was claimed that Dunne had never lost a race. Among his victories were:

- 200-yard dash at the liquor dealers picnic in 1887 and 1889
- Three half mile races at the Grand Army picnic in 1889
- Two quarter mile races at the order of foresters' picnics in 1889, 1890, and 1891
- 100-yard dash, quarter mile and half mile victories over renown sprinter Coughlin on 11/7/1891 at the Varuna Boat Club
- 100-yard dash, 220 yard dash and half mile at the National Athletic Club games of 1892

One goal Dunne yearned for had eluded him, and that was a victory over Eugene Hickey. Hickey was a New York police officer assigned to the Fifteenth Precinct and a runner for the New York Athletic Club. Hickey claimed to be the best runner in New York State and had once challenged any police officer in the state to a race from one to five miles for the New York State championship. Dunne immediately accepted the challenge, but Hickey never responded to Dunne's offer to race. The race was finally set for October 2nd, 1892, at the Union Athletic Club at Bergan Street and Albany Avenue in Brooklyn. At stake was claimed to be the championship of the United States and a gold medal worth fifty dollars.[116]

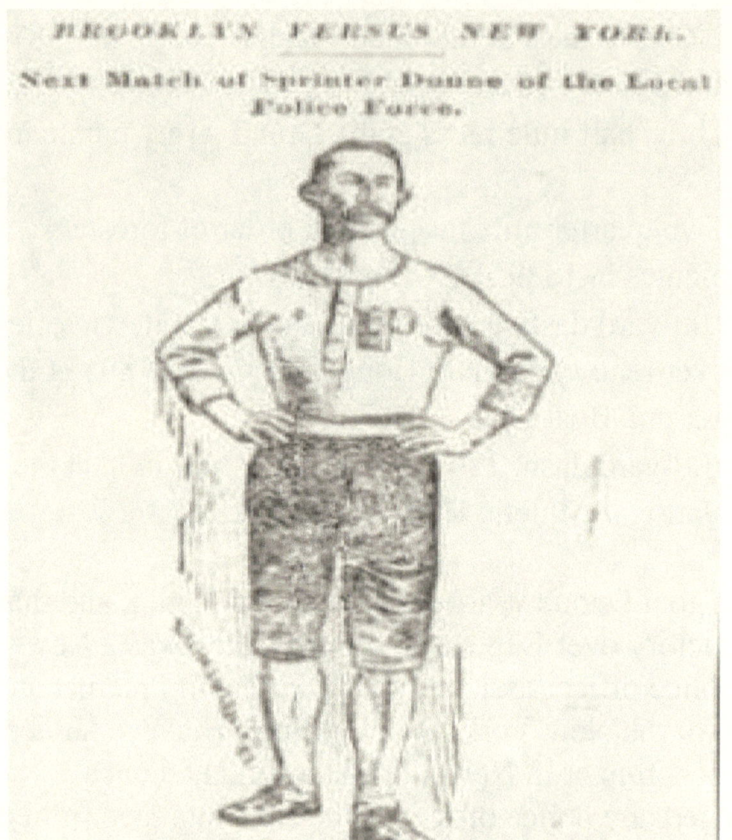

Patrolman Nicholas Dunne

The contestants decided on a mile race, which was eight laps around the Union Athletic Club track. The Brooklyn cops were extremely confident in Dunne before the race, and they had good reason to be. Just a few days earlier Dunne had run a 4:59 mile while the best mile time Hickey had ever recorded was 5:20. Dunne's supporters believed a wager on their man was going to be easy money.

Mysteriously, on the day of the race the odds went from even money to 4 to 1 in favor of Hickey. Members of the New York force confidently wagered large sums of money on Hickey including a detective who flashed a roll of $2,500 to bet.

The race was a disaster for Dunne, who retired after five laps of the eight-lap race. The Brooklyn cops lost a ton of money, and it wasn't long before the dark rumors began to emerge. Maybe there was a reason the New York cops were so confident. Some conspiracy theorists pointed to how strangely Dunne appeared to be acting. After one lap his head swung from side to side, his pace lessened, his arms dropped to his side, and he appeared on the verge of collapse. Some began to claim that Dunne had been drugged. The drug charged could never be substantiated, but those fueling the claim noted that Dunne collapsed on his post the following night and that his trainer, famous sprinter Nicholas Cox, was very friendly with the New York Police – maybe too friendly.[117]

I could find nothing more regarding the alleged drugging of Nicholas Dunne or his rivalry with Eugene Hickey. Perhaps much of the luster of this Brooklyn versus New York rivalry faded in 1898 when the Brooklyn Police Department was consolidated with the New York department and Nicholas Dunne became of member of the new NYPD. I did find one more reference to Dunne in an event twelve years after his race with Hickey that could be considered athletic in which Dunne also emerged as the loser.

On July 27th, 1904, Patrolman Dunne was working an overnight shift in Manhattan, patrolling at 109th Street and Amsterdam Avenue. During the early morning hour he heard a loud noise coming from the direction of 110th Street. As he got closer, Dunne observed Dr. Julius Taylor and Dr. Henry Kellogg, both 27-years old, and both on the staff at St. Luke's Hospital. The source of the noise was the two physicians shaking a lamp post violently. Their actions were such that Dunne later said they looked like monkeys on a stick. As Dunne approached the doctors, one of them picked up a rock and threw it at the top of the lamp post, breaking the globe. Both doctors ran, but Dunne, still possessing a reputation as a great runner, caught them at 111th Street. In retrospect, Dunne probably wished he wasn't such a great runner because he did not fare well in the ensuing battle with the powerfully built doctors. His uniform was torn to shreds and he suffered lacerations to his face, a tooth was knocked out, his lower lip was gashed, and his jaw and entire body was bruised. Thankfully, help arrived, and the doctors received a trip to jail while Dunne received a trip to the sick list.[118]

The Police vs. Reporters.

The Police Baseball Club and the Police Headquarters Reporters' Baseball Club played yesterday afternoon on the grounds of the Brooklyn
Athletic Association, with following result:

```
Reporters.................0 0 1 3 0 0 0 0 0—4
Police....................1 0 0 1 1 0 1 1 .—5
```

The nines were made up as follows: Police—
Golden, 1 b.; Farrell, 3 b.; Rawley, r. f.; Finnegan, 2 b.; Klingman, c.; Alwinck, l. f.; Allison,
c. f.; Lawlor, s. s.; Remills, p.

Reporters—H. Cadmus, 3 b.; Kemble, 1 b.;
McMurray, c.; Moore, 2 b.; Fischer, s. s.; Herries,
l. f.; Sullivan, c. f.; Stoddard, r. f.; W. Cadmus, p.

The nines will play again Sept. 27, when the
reporters will win either in the field or in the
newspapers.

BROOKLYN POLICE WIN.

Beat the Saratogas in a Ball Game, 20 to 6.

The Brooklyn Police Baseball team defeated the Saratogas on the Macon street
grounds yesterday by a score of 20 to 6.
The Saratogas claim that the umpire was
overawed by the official aspect of the cops,
hence the score. At any rate many of the
decisions of the umpire were open to question.

In the first inning the police scored enough
runs to hold the game safe. They used their
bats effectively thereafter, tallying runs in
every inning but two.

A return game will be played on Monday
on the same grounds. Score:

Brooklyn Police	r.	1b.	p.o.	a.	e.	Saratoga B. B. C.	r.	1b.	p.o.	a.	e.
Schaffer, 3b	[illegible]	[illegible]	[illegible]	[illegible]	[illegible]	Feldman, c.f.	[illegible]	[illegible]	[illegible]	[illegible]	[illegible]
Walters, c.f.	[illegible]	[illegible]	[illegible]	[illegible]	[illegible]	M'Auliffe, r.f.	[illegible]	[illegible]	[illegible]	[illegible]	[illegible]
Clare, 1b	[illegible]	[illegible]	[illegible]	[illegible]	[illegible]	Hayes, 3b	[illegible]	[illegible]	[illegible]	[illegible]	[illegible]
Veach, 2b	[illegible]	[illegible]	[illegible]	[illegible]	[illegible]	Young, l.f.	[illegible]	[illegible]	[illegible]	[illegible]	[illegible]
Rowe, s.s.	[illegible]	[illegible]	[illegible]	[illegible]	[illegible]	Evers, p. & 2b.	[illegible]	[illegible]	[illegible]	[illegible]	[illegible]
Madigan, c.	[illegible]	[illegible]	[illegible]	[illegible]	[illegible]	Beck, c.	[illegible]	[illegible]	[illegible]	[illegible]	[illegible]
D'Cantillon, r.f.	[illegible]	[illegible]	[illegible]	[illegible]	[illegible]	Liespenard, s.s.	[illegible]	[illegible]	[illegible]	[illegible]	[illegible]
Lynch, l.f.	[illegible]	[illegible]	[illegible]	[illegible]	[illegible]	Schlosser, 1b	[illegible]	[illegible]	[illegible]	[illegible]	[illegible]
Fritz, p.	[illegible]	[illegible]	[illegible]	[illegible]	[illegible]	Liespenard, p. & 2b.	[illegible]	[illegible]	[illegible]	[illegible]	[illegible]
Howard, p.	[illegible]	[illegible]	[illegible]	[illegible]	[illegible]						
Total	20	[illegible]	[illegible]	17	[illegible]	Total	6	[illegible]	[illegible]	[illegible]	[illegible]

```
                  1 2 3 4 5 6 7 8 9
Brooklyn Police.. [illegible]—20
Saratoga B. B. C. [illegible]—6
```

*Veach and Beck out for interference.

Home runs—Walters. Three base hit—Lynch.
Two base hits—Rowe, Madigan, Do Cantillon,
Feldman, McAuliffe. Struck out—By Fritz, 1;
by Liespenard, 1; by Evers, 1. Bases on balls—Off
Fritz, 1, off Liespenard, 1, off Evers, 2.

THE END OF AN ERA

There was a surreal feeling to the morning. The commanders of the Brooklyn Police Department had attended countless meetings inside police headquarters, but this one was different. It was December 31, 1897, and this would be the last time they would be meeting as member of the police force of the city of Brooklyn. The consolidation of Greater New York City would occur when the new year rolled in, and they expected to receive orders as to what they were to do under the new department.

Superintendent Mackellar directed his commanders to continue with their normal procedures and protocols until such time as new orders were received. He further stated that it was his impression that no new orders could be given until the new Board of Police Commissioners met and appointed an Acting Chief, with that meeting expected to take place sometime on New Year's Day. Police Commissioner Welles had planned on joining the police commanders to bid them farewell, but he was ill at home. Superintendent Mackellar advised that it would be a nice gesture for the captains to visit the commissioner sometime on New Year's Day.[119]

For the people gathered City Hall that evening, there was not the festive mood normally associated with a New Year's Eve party. They met on that miserably cold, rainy night for the "observance" of their city's merger with New York at midnight. They specifically refused to call it a celebration. Brooklyn's Mayor got a long round of applause for his efforts to prevent New York City, which then consisted of just Manhattan and the southwestern Bronx, from annexing its neighbors to create the boroughs of Brooklyn, Queens, the Bronx and Staten Island. The evening's featured speaker was another leader of the resistance, St. Clair McKelway, the editor of The Brooklyn Daily Eagle.

Sharing Manhattan's tax revenues appealed to many Brooklynites (enough, at least, to vote for the merger), but McKelway feared his industrious city would be corrupted by marrying for money. "Brooklyn has repeatedly shown herself to be the most independent urban community in the world," McKelway told the somber audience. "There need be no apology for the poverty of Brooklyn. It is an honorable poverty."

Across the river, Manhattan's merchants, bankers and publishers celebrated their triumph with fireworks and a parade. The Times could not resist gloating. It ridiculed McKelway's speech in an article pretending to share his concern.

Assimilation had occurred. The City of Brooklyn, with its rich, but brief history was gone, along with its police department. But the history of the borough of Brooklyn in the Greater City of New York was just beginning.

Bibliography

1.   Williams, Keith, Brooklyn's Evolution from Small Town to Big City to Borough, Blurred Lines, 7/24/14
2.   FROM HUDSON TO DATE, The Brooklyn Daily Eagle, 10/1/1892, p8
3.   William E.S. Fales, Brooklyn's Guardians, New York, 1887, p2,3
4.   William E.S. Fales, Brooklyn's Guardians, New York, 1887, p6
5.   Sagui, Samantha, The Hue and Cry in Medieval English Towns, Historical Research, 2014, p87
6.   William E.S. Fales, Brooklyn's Guardians, New York, 1887, p7,8
7.   William E.S. Fales, Brooklyn's Guardians, New York, 1887, p21
8.   Williams, Keith, Brooklyn's Evolution from Small Town to Big City to Borough, Blurred Lines, 7/24/14
9.   Williams, Keith, Brooklyn's Evolution from Small Town to Big City to Borough, Blurred Lines, 7/24/14
10.   POLICE! POLICE!, Brooklyn Union, 5/15/1871
11.   William E.S. Fales, Brooklyn's Guardians, New York, 1887, p24
12.   William E.S. Fales, Brooklyn's Guardians, New York, 1887, p25
13.   William E.S. Fales, Brooklyn's Guardians, New York, 1887, p30
14.   William E.S. Fales, Brooklyn's Guardians, New York, 1887, p34-37
15.   POLICE! POLICE!, Brooklyn Union, 5/15/1871
16.   William E.S. Fales, Brooklyn's Guardians, New York, 1887, p37-41
17.   Vocabulary.com
https://www.vocabulary.com/dictionary/precinct

18.   William E.S. Fales, Brooklyn's Guardians, New York, 1887, p37

19.   William E.S. Fales, Brooklyn's Guardians, New York, 1887, p38

20.   HISTORY, New York draft Riots, History.com editors, April 16, 2021 https://www.history.com/topics/american-civil-war/draft-riots

21.   William E.S. Fales, Brooklyn's Guardians, New York, 1887, p42-58

22.   POLICE! POLICE!, Brooklyn Union, 5/15/1871

23.   William E.S. Fales, Brooklyn's Guardians, New York, 1887, p465

24.   Guerra, Emilio, 4th Precinct Station House, Clinton Hill, Brooklyn, United States

25.   THE OTERO MURDER, Harper's Weekly, 12/16/1865, p797

26.   OUR GUARDIANS, The Brooklyn Sunday Sun, 6/25/1876, p3

27.   William E.S. Fales, Brooklyn's Guardians, New York, 1887, p259-271

28.   A VICTIM, The Brooklyn Daily Eagle, 7/6/76, p4

29.   A POLICEMAN SENTENCED, The Brooklyn Union, 8/28/75, p4

30.   POLICE TRIALS, The Brooklyn Daily Eagle, 1/14/75, p3

31.   UNTITLED, The Brooklyn Daily Sun, 11/7/75, p5

32.   THE COURTS, The Brooklyn Union, 11/16/76, p4

33.   THE COURTS, The Brooklyn Union, 11/16/76, p4

34.   OFFICER SCOTT, The Brooklyn Daily Eagle, 10/27/76, p4

35.   OFFICER SCOTT's DEATH, The Brooklyn Union, 7/12/76, p4

36.   ANOTHER MURDER, Brooklyn Times Union, 7/6/76, p4

37.   Loingsigh, Eamon, Gangs of Brooklyn, 2/18/14

38.   A VICTIM, The Brooklyn Daily Eagle, 7/6/76, p4

39.   ANOTHER MURDER, Brooklyn Times Union, 7/6/76, p4

40.   OFFICER SCOTT, The Brooklyn Daily Eagle, 10/27/76, p4

41.   A VICTIM, The Brooklyn Daily Eagle, 7/6/76, p4

42.   OFFICER SCOTT's DEATH, The Brooklyn Union, 7/12/76, p4

43.   OFFICER SCOTT, The Brooklyn Daily eagle, 10/27/76, p4

44.   ANOTHER MURDER, Brooklyn Times Union, 7/6/76, p4

45.   OFFICER SCOTT'S DEATH, The Brooklyn Union, 7/12/76, p4

46.   ANOTHER MURDER, Brooklyn Times Union, 7/6/76, p4

47.   A VICTIM, The Brooklyn Daily Eagle, 7/6/76, p4

48.   ANOTHER MURDER, Brooklyn Times Union, 7/6/76, p4

49.   A VICTIM, The Brooklyn Daily Eagle, 7/6/76, p4

50.   OFFICER SCOTT, The Brooklyn Daily Eagle, 7/10/76, p3

51.   SPOILING FOR A FIGHT, The Brooklyn Daily Eagle, 7/13/76, p4

52.   GETTING SQUARE, The Brooklyn Sunday Sun, 8/13/76, p1

53.   CONFESSION, The Brooklyn Daily Eagle, 7/13/76, p4

54.   HURLEY, The Brooklyn Daily Eagle, 11/1/76, p4

55.   William E.S. Fales, Brooklyn's Guardians, New York, 1887, p54
56.   UNTITLED, The Brooklyn Daily Eagle, 7/11/76 p.3
57.   Casetext: Smarter Legal Research, People ex Rel. Waddy v. Partridge
1902
58.   THE HEAT, The Brooklyn Daily Eagle, 7/10/76, p4
59.   POLICE FUNERALS, Brooklyn Times Union, 7/11/76 p4
60.   Casetext: Smarter Legal Research, People ex Rel. Waddy v. Partridge
1902
61.   AN INSANE POLICEMAN, The Standard Union, 7/25/1898, p2
62.   HIS SANITY IN DOUBT, The Brooklyn Daily Eagle, 7/25/1898, p14
63.   LOFTUS RESTING QUIETLY, The Brooklyn Daily Eagle, 7/27/1898, p8
64.   POLICEMAN LOFTUS' FUNERAL, Brooklyn Times Union, 11/7/1900, p2
65.   HAYDEN AND HIS STAFF, The Brooklyn Daily Eagle, 6/1/1890, p9
66.   William E.S. Fales, Brooklyn's Guardians, New York, 1887, p49
67.   THE GALLOWS, THE BROOKLYN UNION, 12/6/72, p2
68.   Cobb, Geoff, Historical Greenpoint, Bad Boys of the Past, The Notorious Gangs of North Brooklyn, January 9, 2017
69.   THIEF CATCHING, The Brooklyn Daily Eagle, 6/22/1877, p1
70.   RUBENSTEIN, The Brooklyn Daily Eagle, 12/16/1875, p4

71.   RUBENSTEIN, The Brooklyn Daily Eagle, 2/14/1876, p4

72.   William E.S. Fales, Brooklyn's Guardians, New York, 1887, p59

73.   DETECTIVES REWARDED, The Brooklyn Daily Eagle, 5/8/77, P4

74.   A BIG STEAL, THE BROOKLTN UNION, 3/23/77, p4

75.   THE BROOKLYN BANK BOOKKEEPER, Brooklyn Times Union, 3/24/77, p4

76.   FOOLISH BERGHAUSER, Times Union, 1/3/1878, p4

77.   William E.S. Fales, Brooklyn's Guardians, New York, 1887, p231-369

78.   William E.S. Fales, Brooklyn's Guardians, New York, 1887, p413

79.   William E.S. Fales, Brooklyn's Guardians, New York, 1887, p469-471

80.   POLICE DISCIPLINE, The Brooklyn Daily Eagle, 6/20/1878, p3

81.   AN INSANE ACT, Brooklyn Times Union, 5/6/1878, p4

82.   THE SESSIONS, The Brooklyn Daily Eagle, 6/18/1878, p4

83.   EASTERN DISTRICT, The Brooklyn Union, 2/11/1879, p3

84.   William E.S. Fales, Brooklyn's Guardians, New York, 1887, p489

85.   William E.S. Fales, Brooklyn's Guardians, New York, 1887, p175-176

86.   William E.S. Fales, Brooklyn's Guardians, New York, 1887, p177

87.   JAMES M. WOOD, The Brooklyn Daily Eagle, 1/13/24, p9

88.   William E.S. Fales, Brooklyn's Guardians, New York, 1887, p180-183

89.   William E.S. Fales, Brooklyn's Guardians, New York, 1887, p198-200

90.   MOUNTED MEN, The Brooklyn Daily Eagle, 11/9/1882, p4

91.   A POLICEMAN'S SPREE, The Brooklyn Union, 12/15/1882, p4

92.   OFFICER WESSMAN'S CASE DISMISSED, The Brooklyn Union, 12/20/1882, p4

93.   William E.S. Fales, Brooklyn's Guardians, New York, 1887, p204

94.   Guariglia, Matthew, SLATE, Facial recognition Technology is the new Rogues' Gallery, 2/17/20

95.   William E.S. Fales, Brooklyn's Guardians, New York, 1887, p209-210

96.   THE JUDGE MOORE"S QUICK WORK, The Brooklyn Daily Eagle, 11/21/1885, p6

97.   Levitt, Leonard, NYPD Confidential, Power and Corruption in the country's greatest police force, Thomas Dunne Books, 2009, p102

98.   William E.S. Fales, Brooklyn's Guardians, New York, 1887, p515

99.   William E.S. Fales, Brooklyn's Guardians, New York, 1887, p501-506

100. William E.S. Fales, Brooklyn's Guardians, New York, 1887, p509

101. Tebeau, Marc, FIRES AND FIREFIGHTING, Cleveland State University

102. OFFICIAL STATEMENT OF CHIEF ENGINEER NEVINS, The Brooklyn Union, 12/8/76, p4

103.   UNTITLED, Brooklyn Times Union, 12/7/1876, p4
104.   THE TERRIBLE BROOKLYN THEATRE FIRE: WORST DISASTER IN BROOKLYN HISTORY. Bowery Boys, 12/5/21
105.   UNTITLED, Brooklyn Times Union, 12/7/1876, p4
106.   SCENES AT THE MORGUE, The Brooklyn Daily eagle, 12/9/76, p4
107.   A RUFFIAN'S RAGE, The Standard Union. 4/25/1887, p1
108.   BROOKLYN'S POLICE NINE, Brooklyn Times Union, 5/28/1887, p2
109.   COPS TO RESUME PLAYING, The Brooklyn Daily Eagle, 8/10/04, p11
110.   DID NOT PLAY, Brooklyn Times Union, 5/22/1895, p2
111.   HE FAVORS BASEBALL Brooklyn Times Union, 5/10/1888, p1
112.   POLICE VICTORIOUS, The Brooklyn Citizen, 6/5/89, p6-7
113.   BROOKLYN POLICE WIN, The Brooklyn Daily Eagle, 8/20/04, p7
114.   THAT BASEBALL DEFEAT, The Brooklyn Citizen, 8/11/1889, p7
115.   ONE-LEGGED BEGGARS THIS COP'S SPECIALTY, The Standard Union, 7/8/04, p4
116.   BROOKLYN VERSUS NEW YORK, Times Union, 9/3/92, p2
117.   THEY TALK OF DRUGGING, The Times Union, 10/7/92, p1
118.   DOCTORS AND POLICEMEN FIGHT, The Brooklyn Daily Eagle, 7/27/04,p6

119. POLICE COMMANDERS GATHER FOR THE LAST TIME AS BROOKLYNITES, Brooklyn Times Union, 12/31/1897, p1